Around-the-World
COOKY BOOK

Around-the-World
COOKY BOOK

BY

Lois Lintner Sumption

AND

Marguerite Lintner Ashbrook

DOVER PUBLICATIONS, INC.
NEW YORK

Published in Canada by General Publishing Company,
Ltd., 30 Lesmill Road, Don Mills, Toronto, Ontario.
Published in the United Kingdom by Constable and
Company, Ltd., 10 Orange Street, London WC2H 7EG.

This Dover edition, first published in 1979, is an un-
abridged republication of the revised (1948) edition of
the work as published by Chas. A. Bennett Co., Peoria,
Illinois, under the title *Cookies and More Cookies*.

International Standard Book Number: 0-486-23802-4
Library of Congress Catalog Card Number: 78-75141

Manufactured in the United States of America
Dover Publications, Inc.
180 Varick Street
New York, N.Y. 10014

TO

MERLE R. SUMPTION
AND
ROSS SPELMAN ASHBROOK

OUR HUSBANDS WHO HAVE FAITHFULLY TASTED
AND CRITICIZED EACH OF THE KINDS OF COOKIES
AND TO ALL OTHERS
WHO HAVE SO GRACIOUSLY AIDED US

THIS BOOK
IS AFFECTIONATELY DEDICATED
BY THE AUTHORS

CONVERSION TABLES FOR FOREIGN EQUIVALENTS

DRY INGREDIENTS

Ounces	Grams	Grams	Ounces	Pounds	Kilograms	Kilograms	Pounds
1 =	28.35	1 =	0.035	1 =	0.454	1 =	2.205
2	56.70	2	0.07	2	0.91	2	4.41
3	85.05	3	0.11	3	1.36	3	6.61
4	113.40	4	0.14	4	1.81	4	8.82
5	141.75	5	0.18	5	2.27	5	11.02
6	170.10	6	0.21	6	2.72	6	13.23
7	198.45	7	0.25	7	3.18	7	15.43
8	226.80	8	0.28	8	3.63	8	17.64
9	255.15	9	0.32	9	4.08	9	19.84
10	283.50	10	0.35	10	4.54	10	22.05
11	311.85	11	0.39	11	4.99	11	24.26
12	340.20	12	0.42	12	5.44	12	26.46
13	368.55	13	0.46	13	5.90	13	28.67
14	396.90	14	0.49	14	6.35	14	30.87
15	425.25	15	0.53	15	6.81	15	33.08
16	453.60	16	0.57				

LIQUID INGREDIENTS

Liquid Ounces	Milliliters	Milliliters	Liquid Ounces	Quarts	Liters	Liters	Quarts
1 =	29.573	1 =	0.034	1 =	0.946	1 =	1.057
2	59.15	2	0.07	2	1.89	2	2.11
3	88.72	3	0.10	3	2.84	3	3.17
4	118.30	4	0.14	4	3.79	4	4.23
5	147.87	5	0.17	5	4.73	5	5.28
6	177.44	6	0.20	6	5.68	6	6.34
7	207.02	7	0.24	7	6.62	7	7.40
8	236.59	8	0.27	8	7.57	8	8.45
9	266.16	9	0.30	9	8.52	9	9.51
10	295.73	10	0.33	10	9.47	10	10.57

Gallons (American)	Liters	Liters	Gallons (American)
1 =	3.785	1 =	0.264
2	7.57	2	0.53
3	11.36	3	0.79
4	15.14	4	1.06
5	18.93	5	1.32
6	22.71	6	1.59
7	26.50	7	1.85
8	30.28	8	2.11
9	34.07	9	2.38
10	37.86	10	2.74

INTRODUCTION

"And behind our kitchen door there was always a barrel of apples and a large stone cooky jar which was full of cookies. And that's where we children went for our afternoon piece." Many are the times we heard that from our mother. It is little wonder, then, that we early developed more than a mere gustatory interest in cookies.

We collected cookies instead of stamps since we were encouraged to play in real cooky dough rather than the mud-pie kind. Of course we used "enough flour to make them good and tough," but at least it was the beginning of a lasting interest. Years have passed since those days, and at last we have enough recipes to fill a book. We feel that the public—the cooking and eating public—will welcome another recipe book which is, of course, "just another recipe book" but with a difference.

Cooky baking is a special type of activity. When you want to bake cookies, you don't want to look through a big book of recipes. That is the reason we feel that all of our recipes on cookies should be gathered under one cover.

One doesn't want to eat the same type of cooky over and over again. For those families who are victims of "the woman who always makes a batch of sugar cookies," we are, indeed, sorry. This book, therefore, contains an "infinite variety" of recipes which will be found suitable for any occasion and any quirk of appetite. Here are cookies that will appeal to the American taste and to those Americans who have had their roots lately in other lands. Here are those cookies which are easy to make; those which are difficult but worth the time and effort spent in making them; those which are very expensive and those which can be stirred up out of almost nothing; those which appeal to the hungry boy who wants something to "stick to his ribs" and those which will tempt the most jaded appetite.

If you've made cakes all your life and think that cookies are too difficult to bother with, try them. You'll find that it seems true that cake bakers—real cake bakers—are born and not made. The same holds true of pie makers. But the cooky baker can be developed with not much effort. Simply follow the recipe, and if you should make the mistake of deviating a bit, the result is not half as disastrous as that much deviation in a cake. When you are called to the telephone, the cookie dough, half mixed, can wait and not suffer. Not so with a cake.

Cookies will keep much longer than cakes. We make them to have on hand. A cake made to have "on hand" will always be a bit stale. In most instances cookies will fit into your entertainment situation better than cakes or pies. Icebox cookies can be made and baked fresh for each occasion. Some of the honey-and-molasses types are much better after they are a week or two old. So, when company is coming, get the cooky dough ready for immediate and later consumption.

It is true that you can buy good cookies. But in doing so you don't have the great variety. Furthermore, you don't have the fun of making them. Cooky bakings can be real events. Try entertaining with one sometime, especially before Christmas when a great quantity needs to be made. If you don't have an electric beater, the guests at the baking will enjoy taking their turn on the beating. One woman who came to a cooky baking said, sincerely, "I never had so much fun in my life."

You can save money by making cookies. Think what even so inexpensive a thing as a vanilla wafer costs when you buy it at the bakery. A housewife can't count her time as worth much in money; therefore she saves a great deal of money when she bakes the cookies for the bridge party, the dinner dessert, the picnic, and the snack.

We have taken the liberty of changing many of these recipes to suit modern methods. Grandmother made good cookies by a long, roundabout method; but, if we have found a way to make just as good cookies by a short cut, we believe that the short cut is justified.

People say, "Why include so many foreign recipes? Why not 'cook American'?" We answer that we have chosen wherever we have found good recipes, and we have tried to appeal to all types of appetites. Moreover, tastes can be developed. If you don't like *Peppernuts* the first time, try them again and you'll wonder why you deprived yourself of that source of enjoyment so long.

We have learned much about cookies and the interesting customs connected with them since we've been collecting, and we are passing this information to you. Many of the recipes included here have been in use in our family for generations. Some have been contributed by friends who have been interested in the project; others are the authors' inventions; and all have been tested personally by the authors.

HISTORY

Cooky, cookie, or cookey, but the first is preferred, came from the Dutch "koekje," a diminutive of "koek," meaning cake. "In the United States it is usually a small, flat, sweet cake, but locally a name for small cakes of various forms with or without sweetening." Dr. George H. McKnight, of the English department, Ohio State University, says, ". . . I can only say that the English word is usually explained as coming first into American English from the Dutch in New York State. The latest (1934) edition of Webster supports that derivation, and the information in the Oxford Dictionary does not preclude that explanation. In the supplement to the Oxford Dictionary are given some citations of the word from the Dutch of South Africa. I think, therefore, we will award the cooky to the Dutch."

"Cooky-shines," meaning tea parties, are mentioned in 1863 by Reade in *Hard Cash,* and it is known through books to have been a common expression at that time because cookies did so frequently appear at the tea table. This expression is still used, more or less as slang, in some parts of the United States.

It isn't known just when the first cookies came into existence, nor who was the chef who conceived them. Primitive diets didn't include anything so fancy, but mention is made in 1563 in England, in what would correspond to our cookbooks, of *Simnel Cakes* which were small cakes which could not be refused to children who came asking for them on Christmas morning. Sir Kenelm Digby in his famous *Cookery Booke* includes a recipe for:

EXCELLENT SMALL CAKES

"Take three pound of very fine flower well dryed by the fire; and put to it a pound and a half of loaf sugar sifted in a very fine sieve and dryed; Three pounds of Currants well washed and dryed in a cloth and set by the fire; when your flower is well mixed with the sugar and currants, you must put in it a pound and a half of unmelted butter, 10 spoonfuls of cream, with the yolks of three new-layd eggs beat with it, one nutmeg; and if you please, three spoonfuls of Sack. When you have wrought your paste well, you must put it in a cloth and set it in a dish before the fire, till it be through warm. Then make them up in little cakes and prick them full of holes; you must bake them in a quick oven unclosed. Afterwards, ice them over with sugar. The cakes should be about the bigness of a handbreadth and thin; of the cise of the sugar cakes sold at Barnet."

Funny old recipes they are, and difficult for the modern person of to-day to follow. Even the modern foreign recipes are a bit difficult to understand. We wonder why they call for so very many eggs, and we soon find that eggs were the leavening agent before the time of baking powder and soda, and that many of these old-time recipes remain in use. One Hungarian woman, who was telling of some of her pet recipes, said, "We believe in making a thing good, and you can't cook good baking without lots of eggs, so we use them."

One American woman, in looking over a number of foreign recipes of to-day, exclaimed, "Goodness! Don't they ever use any nuts except almonds? They're too expensive for me." It is true that the almond is very common in foreign cookery, especially in France, Germany, and Spain where that is a native nut. The chestnut is common in Italian recipes for the same reason, and the pistachio in countries close to the Mediterranean. Each country uses what it has most plentifully and close at hand, and therefore produces dishes with a so-called characteristic flavor. If we are to attempt to appreciate the culture of that country, we must use that which is typical of it.

But interesting as it is to learn of the background of the recipes, the origin of the word, the characteristic products of each country, it is far more interesting to come at once to the thing represented by a cookery book—food and the taste thereof. As Dr. McKnight says, "I think there are features of the cooky more interesting than the derivation of its name, and you could doubtless tell me all about that."

CONTENTS

11

MAYBE YOU WOULD LIKE TO TRY THESE

HINTS AND SUGGESTIONS

1. Kinds of cookies.—There are two general kinds of cookies just as there are two general kinds of cakes. One uses butter; the other, sponge type, uses eggs.

2. When to serve cookies.—Certain kinds are better adapted to combination with one thing rather than another. This has been indicated in each recipe where it is of sufficient importance to be noted. Some cracker-like types would be fine with certain types of beverages, while others are so rich that they would be entirely *de trop* with a rich dessert. Where no suggestions are made, the cooky may be served in any combination with good results.

3. Methods of making.—Certain mixtures lend themselves best to a special method, but in many cases changes may be made. A dropped cooky could be spread and a rolled cooky could follow the icebox method.

A. *Dropped.*—This is an easy method where the mixture is dropped from the tip of a teaspoon an inch apart. If the dough is stiff enough, balls may be formed with the hands and flattened with a knife or the tines of a fork. With a thinner batter, the mass may be spread over a cooky sheet and marked in squares or bars while still warm.

B. *Filled.*—Any rolled cooky may be put together with a great variety of fillings, sandwich fashion; or a spoonful of filling may be put on one side of a large, round cooky and the other side folded over, the edges pressed

21

together and the top pricked. Squares may be folded to make tricorns.

C. *Rolled.*—This is the old and well-known method where the mixture is rolled thin and cut in plain and fancy shapes. Great care must be taken to keep the dough cool, working with only a part of it at a time so that extra flour will not have to be added and thus make the cooky tough. Keep the part you are not working with in a cold place.

D. *Icebox.*—These are very popular because of their ease of making, baking, and serving. The dough is formed into a roll which is covered with waxed paper and chilled over night. The cookies are sliced very thin and are easy to handle. If icebox molds are available, the dough is forced into them, and the same procedure is followed. They have only the advantage of giving fancy shapes. A quantity of this dough may be made up at one time, put in the icebox, and used as desired.

4. Keeping cookies.

A. *Stone jar.*—This is best if a moist cooky is desired. In the jar keep a piece of fresh bread, an apple, or an orange, to insure sufficient moisture and add to the flavor of the cookies. This applies to many German Christmas recipes.

B. *Tin containers.*—Ordinary coffee cans which close tightly are very good containers in which to keep the crisp cooky. If a crisp, wafer-like type should soften, dry it out in the oven.

5. Removal from pans.—All cookies should be removed from the pan as soon as they come from the oven, unless otherwise stated.

6. Greasing.—If you keep handy a tall, slim jar, like an olive jar, about a fourth full of cooking oil, with a brush in it to be used for greasing, you will find that the greasing of cooky sheets is not a problem. Remember never to use butter to grease pans as it causes things to stick.

7. All chocolate should be melted over water as it burns very easily. One square equals one ounce.

8. Remember that some of the cookies in this book will not be liked by all people. This is especially true of a few from foreign countries which are vastly different in texture or flavor from those to which we are accustomed. A cooky may be a perfect representative of its type and yet you may not like it.

9. If you are limited in time, make a cooky which does not require rolling, as that is a lengthy process.

10. All cookies should be baked on a cooky sheet, as high-sided pans prevent quick browning. Exceptions are noted in specific recipes.

11. It is well to have a roll of some kind of icebox cooky in the icebox ready for quick entertaining.

I. NECESSARY

1. Set of mixing bowls in assorted sizes.

2. Rotary egg beater.

3. Set of assorted measuring spoons.

4. Set of assorted measuring cups, or two of one-cup size, with divisional marks to indicate fractional quantities. Time will be saved if one set is kept for liquid and one for dry measuring.

5. Case knife for leveling measurements.

6. Sharp knife for paring.

7. Spatulas—one broad; the other small; and both should be quite flexible in order to slide under the cooky easily.

8. Rolling pin.

9. Board for rolling.

10. Cooky sheets, square cake pan, and small muffin pans.

II. NOT ESSENTIAL BUT FINE TO HAVE

1. Small grinder for fruits and nuts.

2. Set of fancy cooky cutters (glass, or can top, especially baking-powder top, may be used).

3. Icebox molds (butter carton or waxed paper may be used).

4. Electric mixer (saves time and energy).

5. Springerle board or pin.

6. Pastry mixer (knives may be used).

7. Brush for greasing pans.

8. Cooky press with pastry tube attachment.

9. Candy thermometer.

10. Oven thermometer.

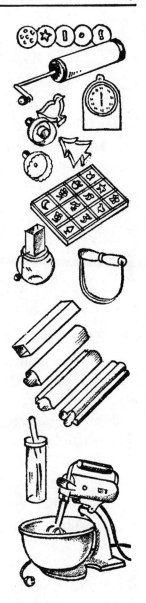

HOW TO USE THIS BOOK

Each of these recipes has been tested according to the following rules, which should be adhered to for perfect results:

1. Key to the symbols:

B.P. . . . . baking powder

B. sugar . . . . brown sugar

C. sugar . . . . confectioner's sugar

G. sugar . . . . granulated sugar

c . . . . cup

t . . . . teaspoonful

T . . . . tablespoonful

f.g. . . . . few grains

2. All measurements are level. This is very important!

3. All flour is sifted once before measuring. If more sifting is required, this is noted in the recipe. Bread flour is used unless pastry flour is indicated. Pastry flour may be made by substituting one tablespoonful of cornstarch for one tablespoonful of bread flour in each cup.

To measure flour, put the sifted flour into a measure, care being taken not to pack it down. Level it off with the straight edge of a knife. Coarse flours, as whole wheat, corn meal, etc., are measured in the same way, but do not need to be sifted.

4. All sugar is granulated unless otherwise specified. It is not necessary to sift any sugar. Measure it as for flour, except B. sugar, which should be packed firmly into the meas-

ure. If C. sugar contains lumps, roll them out before measuring. Molasses and syrup can not be substituted for sugar because of the excess liquid they contain. To measure, put them into a measure and level off with the sharp edge of a knife, because their density tends to make them bulge over the top of the measure.

5. All shortening admits the use of any solidified fat as butter, lard, margarine, etc., unless butter is specified. Even if butter is specified, in the interests of economy one half of the amount of butter may be replaced with the same amount of a butter substitute, plus $\frac{1}{8}$ t to $\frac{1}{4}$ t extra of salt, with only slight changes in flavor and texture, but the product is still very good.

6. All milk is sweet unless otherwise specified, but in any case one-half evaporated milk and one-half water may be substituted for sweet milk. Evaporated milk must not be confused with condensed milk which is very thick and sweetened. Special mention is made if condensed milk is to be used.

7. All fruit and nuts are added to the dry ingredients, already sifted together, and no extra amount of flour is needed to flour them. Where nuts are used as flour in a recipe, do not substitute one kind for another because they absorb different amounts of liquid. Where they are used only for flavor, they may be used interchangeably.

8. All baking tests were made in a gas oven in which an ordinary thermometer was used, but the terms "moderate," etc., are given because many people do not have oven thermometers. Those who do should translate the terms into degrees according to the chart of their own particular oven.

Remember that very small cookies will bake much faster than large ones; therefore, you may have to decrease or increase the baking time given in each recipe to suit the size of the cooky you have made. In any case, the cookies will not be harmed if you "peek" into the oven to see how they are doing.

9. The number of cookies that a recipe will make is not given because sizes vary in accordance to the fancy of the cook. Such a statement as, "This amount will make three dozen cookies" will be found to be misleading.

10. The size of the egg used will influence the product of a recipe. A very large egg makes too much liquid and a small egg, too little. Recipes in this book were tested with eggs measuring 4 T to the egg if slightly beaten and ¼ c to the egg if unbeaten. It is not necessary to beat the egg unless it is indicated in the recipe.

11. Baking Temperature:

Very slow oven..................	250° F.
Slow oven	300° F.
Moderately slow oven............	325° F.
Moderate oven	350° F.
Moderately hot oven............	375° F.
Hot oven	400° F.
Very hot oven...................450°-500° F.	

★ ★ ★ AMERICA ★ ★ ★

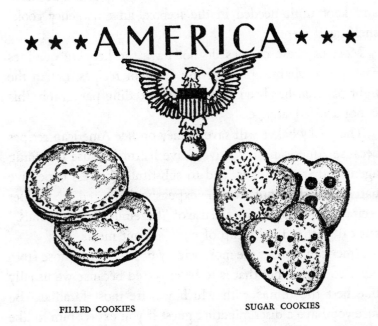

FILLED COOKIES   SUGAR COOKIES

In the matter of cookies as well as in other things America has borrowed as she has pleased from the other nations. She has also invented her own varieties. We find, as we would expect, a blend of characteristics which gives us delicious things that run the gamut from mincemeat to pineapple. Here is the macaroon of France, the seed cooky of Germany, the honey cooky of Holland; but here is also the use of much original material—the gumdrop, apple sauce, pumpkin, banana—all of which are employed to give the touch of originality. And with excellent results!

In general these cookies are simple in method of making, as may be expected of an America accustomed to short cuts. A batch can be made and baked at once, or it can be made and kept until needed in the icebox, an emergency cooky shelf, as it were.

Most of these cookies do not have the keeping qualities that are so characteristic of the German recipes, but in the light of what has been said in the preceding paragraph, this is not a disadvantage.

The cooky baker will save money on her American recipes because American housewives have learned to use leavening agents other than eggs, and to substitute the less expensive native American nuts for the expensive imported types. Her recipes don't insist upon the use of "hazelnuts" or "almonds," but call rather for "1 cup of chopped nut meats."

American cookies are more widely popular than those from other countries, but that is to be expected because we usually like best the things with which we are most familiar. Be sure you have a discriminating guest if you expect him to like *Peppernuts.* But serve an icebox cooky to anybody and you may be sure that he will be pleased.

Brownies

BROWNIES (Plain)

3 T butter	2 eggs
1 c sugar	½ cup flour
1 T cocoa (1 square melted chocolate)	1 c chopped nut meats
	1 t vanilla

Cream the butter and sugar; add the cocoa and beaten eggs. Beat well. Add the flour and vanilla. Spread thin on a greased square pan. Sprinkle thickly with the nuts, and bake in a slow

oven 20–30 minutes. Cut in squares while still warm, and remove
from the pan.

These are rich but delicious and may be served with anything
not too rich in itself.

Betty Walker Pruitt, Columbus, Ohio.

BROWNIES (Chewy)

2 eggs	2 squares chocolate
1¼ c B. sugar	1 c nut meats
½ c flour	1 t vanilla

Beat the eggs; add the sugar, vanilla, and melted chocolate.
Add the flour and half the nuts. Spread on a square pan a half
inch thick and sprinkle the rest of the
nuts on top. Bake in a moderate oven
20–25 minutes. Cut in squares.

This makes a chewy Brownie which
is most liked by some. It is best
adapted to the popular dessert —
Brownies with ice cream and chocolate
sauce on top—because it is much less
likely than the crisp Brownie to fly off
the plate when attacked with a fork!

BROWNIES

NOTE.—The absence of butter causes the chewiness.

BROWNIES (Crisp)

⅓ c butter	½ t vanilla
2 squares chocolate	1 c flour
1 c sugar	½ t B.P.
2 eggs	½ c English walnuts

Sift the dry ingredients. Melt the chocolate; add the butter,
the sugar and the well-beaten eggs and add this mixture to the
flour. Stir in the vanilla and nuts. Pour into a square pan, and
bake 30 minutes in a moderate oven. Mark in squares while still
warm.

BROWNIES (Nonchocolate)

⅓ c butter	1 egg
⅓ c dark corn syrup	¾ c flour
⅓ c B. sugar	¾ c nuts

Cream the butter and sugar; add the corn syrup, the well-beaten egg, the flour, and last, the nuts. Pour in a square pan, and bake in a moderate oven 20–25 minutes. Cut in squares.

These are chewy, have a butterscotch flavor, and are fine for those who don't care for, or are tired of, the chocolate flavor.

BROWNIES (Superfine)

2 squares bitter chocolate	1 c flour
½ c butter	2 t vanilla
1 c sugar	1 c nuts
2 eggs	

Melt the sugar, butter, and chocolate in a double boiler; pour this slowly over the well-beaten eggs. Add the flour and vanilla. Spread over a greased and floured square pan, and sprinkle with nuts. Bake 20–25 minutes in a moderate oven. Cut in squares.

Brownie Jones, Cleveland, Ohio.

Condensed Milk Cookies

APRICOT-PEANUT COOKIES

1½ c sweetened condensed milk	2 T lemon juice
3 c shelled, ground peanuts	1 c ground, dried apricots

Blend all with the milk. Drop on a greased cooky sheet, and bake in a moderate oven 20 minutes. Remove at once from the pan.

These are unusual in flavor and keep fairly well.

CO-CHO-CONS

1 can sweetened
 . condensed milk (1⅓ c)
4 squares chocolate
2 c shredded coconut

f.g. salt
1 t vanilla
3 T flour

Melt the chocolate and stir in the rest of the ingredients. Chill.
Drop from teaspoon on a greased and floured cooky sheet, and
bake in a moderate oven 15 minutes. Watch to prevent burning.
These are delicious and especially nice at "fancy" refreshment
parties.

CO-CHO-CON (with Variations)

Cereal: Omit the chocolate and replace 1 c of the coconut
with 1 c of any popular cereal as corn flakes, bran flakes, or rice
crispies.

Fruit: Omit the chocolate and add ½ c currants, raisins,
chopped dried prunes, stiff pear conserve, dates, figs, etc.

Mrs. Diana Taylor France, Columbus, Ohio.

Crumb Cookies

CHOCOLATE CRUMB COOKIES

1 c evaporated milk
1 square chocolate
1¼ c cake crumbs
 (or graham cracker)

½ t vanilla
¼ t salt
½ c chopped nuts
⅜ c sugar

Cook the milk and the chocolate in a heavy pan until the mixture thickens (about 4 minutes). Add the salt and sugar and cool.
Add the crumbs, nuts, and vanilla. Drop by teaspoonfuls on a
greased cooky sheet, and bake in a moderate oven 10 minutes.

HERMIT CRUMB BARS

¼ c shortening
½ c B. sugar
½ c light corn syrup
2 eggs
½ c finely cut peel
 (or coconut)
½ c raisins
½ t soda

1½ c flour
2 t cinnamon
1 t each allspice, nutmeg,
 and cloves
½ t B.P.
½ t salt
1½ c fine cake crumbs
 (or graham cracker)

Cream the shortening; add the sugar, and cream again. Add the beaten eggs and the corn syrup. Add the sifted-together, dry ingredients. Mix in the cake crumbs, peel, and raisins. Spread thin on a greased cooky sheet, and bake in a moderate oven 10 minutes. Dust with C. sugar, and cut in bars.

Date Cookies

ALABAMA DATE SURPRISES

2 c flour	3 T melted butter
3 t B.P.	1 beaten egg
½ t salt	⅓ c milk
2 T sugar	1 slightly beaten egg white
	for glaze

Sift the dry ingredients. Add the remaining ingredients to form a soft dough. Roll thin (handle as little as possible) and cover individual dates which have been pitted and stuffed with a nut meat, as a half pecan or English walnut. Be sure that each part of the date is covered with dough. Glaze with egg white, and bake in a moderate oven 20 minutes. Be sure that the cookies do not touch each other.

These are fine alone, with a fruit drink, with a salad, with coffee; but they do not keep fresh long and should be used soon after baking.

Helen H. Frankenburg, Columbus, Ohio.

DATE NUT BARS

2 eggs	1¼ c chopped nut meats
½ c sugar	1¼ c chopped dates
5 T flour	1 t B.P.

Beat the eggs; add the sugar, flour and B.P. Stir well. Add the nuts and dates and spread the batter thin on a greased square pan. Bake in a moderate oven 15–20 minutes. Mark in strips while still warm. Remove from the pan and sprinkle with C. sugar.

These are tender but chewy, well liked, and will keep well.

Mrs. H. LaFevre, Fredericktown, Ohio.

DATE NUT ROCKS

1½ c sugar	½ t allspice
1 c butter	1 t soda in 2 t warm water
1½ c chopped nut meats	3 eggs
1 c chopped dates	2½ c flour
1 t cinnamon	

Cream the butter and sugar and add the beaten eggs. Add the sifted-together, dry ingredients to which the fruit and nuts have been added. Last, stir in the soda and warm water. Drop by spoonfuls on a greased cooky sheet, and bake in a moderate oven 10 minutes.

These will keep two or three weeks if stored in a covered tin.

Mrs. Mary Lintner Lewis, Rio Grande, Ohio.

DATE STRIPS

(1)

1 lb. chopped dates (2 c)	1 c boiling water
1 t soda	

Cook for 1 minute.

(2)

1 c sugar	1 t B.P.
1 T melted butter	1 c chopped nuts
1⅓ c flour	Grated rind of ½ lemon

Add 2 to 1 and bake in a long greased pan 15–20 minutes in a moderate oven. Sprinkle with C. sugar mixed with grated orange and lemon rind. Cut in long strips.

These will keep.

Mrs. Mary Lintner Lewis, Rio Grande, Ohio.

Filled Cookies

BASIC RECIPE FOR FILLED COOKIES

½ c shortening	2½–3 c flour
1 c sugar	1½ t B.P.
1 egg	¼ t soda
½ c milk	1 t vanilla

Cream the shortening; add the sugar and the unbeaten egg. Beat well. Add the vanilla and the sifted-together, dry ingredients alter-

nately with the milk. Keep the part of the dough you are not working with cold. Roll thin. Cut in rounds. Put two together with a
spoonful of filling between. Press the edges together (it is best to
moisten them a bit with water too). Prick the tops with a fork.
Bake on a greased cooky sheet in a moderate oven 10 minutes.

Filled cookies should be used soon after they are made as they
do not keep well.

FILLINGS FOR FILLED COOKIES
Cottage Cheese

1 c cottage cheese	¼ t grated lemon rind
4 T currants	1 T chopped nuts
4 T sugar	1 T coconut
¼ t cinnamon	2 T brandy or fruit juice
¼ t nutmeg	1 egg

Blend all together.

Pineapple

2 t cornstarch	½ c crushed pineapple
½ c sugar	(drained)
	½ t lemon juice

Cook all together till thick. Cool before using.

Raisin

1 c raisins	½ c water
½ c sugar	1 t lemon juice
½ c chopped nuts	1 T flour

Mix all and boil until thick. Cool before using. Coconut, grape-
nuts, bran, candied peel may be substituted for the nuts; dates,
currants, figs, apricots, or prunes may be substituted for the raisins.

CHEESE DATE SURPRISES
DOUGH

½ c butter	2 c flour
1 package Philadelphia	
cream cheese	

Cream the warmed butter and cheese together. Add the flour to
form a dough. Chill over night. Roll out thin and cut in three-inch

rounds. Place a spoonful of the filling on one side of the round. Fold the other half over and press the edges together. Prick the top. Bake on a greased cooky sheet in a hot oven 12–15 minutes.

These are delightful with salad.

FILLING

½ c hot water	1 c chopped dates
½ c sugar	2 t lemon juice

Cook slowly together, stirring frequently, until thick.

SPICY CHEESIES

¼ lb. American cream cheese (1c grated)	Cinnamon and C. sugar for sprinkling
¼ c butter	Jelly or conserve
1 c flour	

Cream the warmed butter and the grated cheese. Add the flour. Roll thin. Cut in rounds. Put two rounds together with a spoonful of jelly or conserve, press the edges together. Prick the tops, sprinkle with cinnamon and sugar, and bake in a hot oven 8–10 minutes.

These are good with a fruit salad, beverages, or a fruit dessert. They should be used soon after baking as they do not keep well.

Ginger Cookies

GINGER POUND CAKES

½ c shortening	2 c flour
1 c sugar	½ t B.P.
2 eggs	½ t each cloves, cinnamon,
½ c sorghum or dark molasses	salt
½ t soda	1 T ginger
	½ c sour milk

Cream the shortening; add the sugar, beaten eggs, molasses and soda. Add the sifted-together, dry ingredients alternately with the sour milk. Bake in very small, greased, gem tins in moderate oven 15 minutes. Decorate with a strip of candied peel or preserved ginger before baking, or glaze with lemon glaze after baking. They are excellent without decoration.

Mary Stonestreet Lintner, Leesburg, Virginia.

OLD-FASHIONED GINGER COOKIES

2 c Orleans or Sorghum molasses	1 c sour milk
1 c lard	1½ c sugar
1 t soda	1 t ginger
½ t salt	Flour, enough to roll

Warm the molasses. Add the lard and sugar. Stir well and add the ginger and salt. Mix the soda with the sour milk and add. Use enough flour to form a dough which can be rolled thin. Cut as desired and bake on a greased, floured cooky sheet in a moderate oven 10 minutes. Watch closely to prevent burning. These are just what the name implies.

Mrs. Walter Erlanbach, New Albany, Ohio.

SNAPPIES—Ginger Snaps That Snap!

4 T shortening	1 T vinegar
¼ c B. sugar	1 t soda
1 c Orleans molasses	¼ t each, cinnamon, cloves
2 T hot water	and ginger
	Flour

Warm the molasses and add the shortening, hot water, vinegar, and soda. Add the sugar, spice, and enough flour to roll thin. Cut and bake in a moderate oven 10 minutes.

Icebox Cookies

BUTTERSCOTCH

1 c butter	¼ t salt
2 c B. sugar	3½ c flour
2 eggs	1 c chopped nut meats
½ t soda (beaten in the eggs)	

Cream the butter and sugar; add the rest of the ingredients in the order in which they are listed. Work into a roll or force into icebox cooky molds. Let them stand in the icebox over night. Slice thin, and bake on a greased cooky sheet in a moderate oven 12 minutes.

These have a wonderful butterscotch, nut flavor, and are equally good alone or served with any dessert, especially ice cream. They are a favorite at bridge parties if molded in bridge molds.

Juanita B. Jones, Cleveland, Ohio.

BRAN ICEBOX COOKIES

⅝ c butter	1½ c flour
1 c B. sugar	1 t B.P.
½ c all bran	½ orange rind, grated
1 egg	

Cream the butter; add the sugar and the beaten egg. Add the remaining ingredients and mix well. Form into a long roll and chill overnight. Slice thin and bake in a hot oven about 10 minutes.

Good and good for you!

CHECKERBOARDS

¾ c shortening	1 t B.P.
1 c sugar	¼ t soda
2 eggs	¼ t salt
1 t vanilla	1½ squares melted chocolate
2½ c flour	

Cream the shortening; add the sugar, the beaten eggs, the vanilla, and then the sifted-together, dry ingredients. Divide the dough in half. To one half add the chocolate. Chill both halves. Then form into four long strips, making the sides square. Brush the surface with milk so they will stick together, and on top

CHECKERBOARD

place a dark and white roll, alternating with the white and dark strip below, thus forming a checkerboard. Chill overnight. Slice thin, and bake on a greased cooky sheet in a moderate oven 10 minutes.

Care must be taken to keep the roll square or the checkerboard will not look perfect. This is not so difficult to make, and the pretty effect is worth the bit of extra labor.

FIG-RAISIN COOKIES

1 c shortening	3 t B.P.
2 c B. sugar	1 c coconut
3 eggs	4½ c flour
2 T cream or undiluted evaporated milk	½ t salt
	1 t cinnamon
¾ c chopped, stewed figs	½ t each cloves and nutmeg
1 c seedless raisins	1 t soda

Cream the shortening and the sugar; add the cream and the beaten eggs. Add the sifted-together, dry ingredients, the coco-

nut, figs, and raisins. Shape in a roll and chill overnight. Slice thin, and bake on a greased cooky sheet in a moderate oven 10–12 minutes.

This makes a large quantity. One third of the recipe is a good amount for two to three people. The large amount is practical, however, as the unbaked dough keeps well in the icebox and you have it on hand for some other time.

ICEBOX COOKIES

FRUIT ICEBOX COOKIES

½ c shortening	½ t nutmeg
½ c B. sugar	⅛ t salt
½ c G. sugar	½ c chopped figs
1 egg	½ c chopped raisins
2 T sour cream	¼ c chopped peel
1 t cinnamon	2¼ c flour
½ t cloves	½ t soda

Cream the shortening and sugar. Add the unbeaten egg and the sour cream. Add the rest of the ingredients and shape into two rolls two inches in diameter, or force into icebox molds. Chill overnight. Slice thin, and bake in a moderate oven on a greased cooky sheet 10 minutes.

These are crisp and fine flavored.

LEMON ICEBOX COOKIES

½ c butter	1 T lemon juice
1 c sugar	2 c flour
1 egg	1 t B.P.
1½ t lemon rind, grated	f.g. salt

Cream the butter and sugar; add the well-beaten egg, the lemon juice and rind. Add the sifted-together, dry ingredients. Shape into a roll. Chill overnight. Slice thin, and bake 10 minutes on a greased cooky sheet in a hot oven.

These are tart and nice with a rich dessert.

MINCEMEAT COOKIES

⅔ c B. sugar	1 t cinnamon
⅔ c G. sugar	½ t nutmeg
⅔ c shortening	1 package dry mincemeat
2 beaten eggs	3 c flour
⅓ t soda	

Mix in the order given and form into long rolls or force into icebox molds. Chill overnight. Slice thin, and bake on a greased cooky sheet in a hot oven 10–12 minutes.

These are crisp and spicy. Very nice at holiday time.

RAINBOW ICEBOX COOKIES

½ c butter	1½ c flour
½ c sugar	1 t B.P.
1 T milk	⅛ t salt
1 egg	Coloring
1 t vanilla	

Mix in order given. Divide the dough in half. Add color to one half. Roll out each half separately. Place one half on the other; roll once to make two sheets stick together. Then roll as a jelly roll with the colored part on the inside. Chill overnight. Slice thin, and bake in a moderate oven 12–15 minutes.

These are good and especially attractive for the tea assortment or with a frozen dessert. This amount makes a large quantity.

Macaroons

CORN FLAKE
(1)

2 beaten eggs	½ t vanilla

(2)

1 c sugar	1 c chopped nut meats
3 c corn flakes	f.g. salt
1 c coconut	

Pour 1 over 2. Work gently together. Bake two inches apart in two-inch wide flat cookies on a greased cooky sheet, 18 minutes in a moderate oven.

These are a delicious, chewy, macaroon-like cooky, good alone or with any dessert.

Martha Bethel, Columbus, Ohio.

HICKORY NUT

1 c chopped nuts	½ c sifted C. sugar
1 egg	½ t vanilla
2 T flour	

Beat the egg until very light. Add the rest of the ingredients. Drop by teaspoonfuls on a greased, floured, cooky sheet, and bake in a slow oven 15 minutes. Remove at once and be careful not to crush.

POP CORN

1 c popped corn	f.g. salt
1 T melted butter	½ t vanilla
1 egg white	⅓ c chopped nuts
⅓ c sugar	

Beat the egg white with the salt until it is stiff. Add the sugar and vanilla, beating slowly all the while. Fold in the pop corn and nuts which have been mixed with the butter. Drop by tea-spoonfuls, one inch apart, on a greased cooky sheet. Bake in a slow oven until brown.

These are much like *Corn Flake Macaroons* but with the good flavor of pop corn. They should be used soon after baking as they do not keep well.

Marguerites

PEANUT

Saltines	Peanut butter
Peanuts	Marshmallows

Spread the saltines with peanut butter. Press on the top a half marshmallow and on top of that a peanut. Put under a low broiler flame until the marshmallow is delicately brown. Don't let it burn!

These make a good "hurry up" dessert, a bite with coffee when you have nothing prepared and company drops in, or a good "late at night" snack.

Mrs. Nelle Palmer, Lakewood, Ohio.

PECAN

2 slightly beaten eggs	$\frac{1}{3}$ t salt
1 c B. sugar	1 c chopped pecans
$\frac{1}{2}$ c flour	$\frac{1}{4}$ t B.P.

Mix in order given. Fill small greased and floured muffin tins two thirds full. Place a pecan on top of each cake. Bake in a moderate oven 8–15 minutes.

These are good and chewy, and will keep well in a covered tin.

PLAIN MARGUERITES

$1\frac{1}{2}$ c sugar	2 T coconut
$\frac{1}{2}$ c water	$\frac{1}{4}$ t vanilla
5 marshmallows	1 c chopped walnuts
2 egg whites	Saltines

Boil the water and sugar till it spins a thread. Add the marsh-mallows, finely cut. Pour slowly on the stiffly beaten egg whites.

Add the remaining ingredients. Spread on saltines, and bake in a moderate oven until they dry. Use at once.

Maple Cookies

NUT BARS

½ c butter	2¼ c pastry flour
1 c sugar	f.g. salt
⅝ c maple syrup	2½ t B.P.
3 egg yolks	½ c chopped nut meats
1 T milk	

Cream the butter and add the sugar and syrup. Beat in the egg yolks one at a time and add the milk. Add the sifted-together, dry ingredients and the nuts. Spread evenly in a shallow, greased pan. Cover with frosting, and bake in a moderate oven 30 minutes. Cut in bars while still warm and use while fresh as they do not keep well.

They have a wonderful flavor.

FROSTING

3 egg whites	¼ c maple syrup
1 c sugar	

Beat the egg whites and add slowly the sugar and syrup.

MAPLE NUT HERMITS

1 c shortening	3 c flour
1½ c B. sugar	1 t each cloves, cinnamon,
3 T maple syrup	mace
3 beaten eggs	1 t soda
1 T grated lemon rind	½ t salt
1 c each chopped nuts,	
raisins, dates	

Cream the shortening and sugar. Add the rest, the dry ingredients having been sifted together. Drop by spoonfuls on a greased cooky sheet and bake in a moderate oven 15-20 minutes.

DROPS

⅓ c honey or maple syrup	⅔ c flour
1 T butter	1 t B.P.
1 well-beaten egg	f.g. salt

Cream the butter; add the honey or maple syrup and then the egg. Add the dry ingredients and drop, two inches apart, on a well-greased cooky sheet. Bake in a moderate oven 10–15 minutes.

These are better if iced or glazed and decorated with a piece of nut.

SUGAR COOKIES

1 c crushed maple sugar	2 eggs
1 c G. sugar	2 T water
1 c butter	4 c flour
2 t B.P.	

Cream the butter and the sugar. Add the beaten eggs and the rest of the ingredients. This should form a soft dough which may be either rolled and cut or spread in a square, greased pan and marked as it comes from the oven. In either case bake in a moderate oven about 15 minutes.

These are much like the usual sugar cooky but with the wonderful flavor of maple sugar.

Miscellaneous

BRAN HERMITS

1 c B. sugar	2 c flour
1 c shortening	2 t B.P.
1 egg	½ c chopped nuts
½ c sour milk	½ c chopped raisins
½ t salt	½ c chopped dates or figs,
½ t soda	or both
1 t vanilla	½ t cinnamon
1 c all bran	

Cream the shortening and sugar. Add the unbeaten egg, the sour milk, and the vanilla; then the sifted-together dry ingredients; the fruit, bran, and nuts. Drop from a teaspoon, one inch apart, on a greased cooky sheet. Bake in a moderate oven 12–15 minutes.

These are fine for persons who need a bran regulator, and are well adapted to children who love them but have no idea that they are a "medicinal" cooky. They taste good and keep well.

BUTTERSCOTCH DROP COOKIES

⅔ c butter	2 c flour
1 c B. sugar	2 t B.P.
4 egg yolks or 2 whole eggs	¼ c milk
	½ c coconut

Cream the butter; add the sugar and beaten eggs. Add the sifted-together, dry ingredients alternately with the milk. Add the coconut. Drop by teaspoonfuls on a greased cooky sheet an inch apart. Bake in a moderate oven 10–12 minutes. Nuts may be substituted for the coconut, but the latter gives a special flavor.

CHOCOLATE DROP COOKIES

½ c shortening	¼ t salt
1 c light B. sugar	1 square chocolate or
1 egg	¼ c cocoa
½ c milk	1 c chopped nuts
1½ c flour	1 t vanilla
½ t soda	

Cream the shortening; add the sugar and the well-beaten egg. Add the sifted-together, dry ingredients alternately with the milk. Stir in the melted chocolate, the vanilla, and the nuts. Bake on a greased cooky sheet 10 minutes.

These are excellent and easy to make. They may be kept and iced as needed with any chocolate icing.

COCONUT KISSES

½ c evaporated milk	2 c shredded coconut
½ c sugar	½ t vanilla
⅛ lb. German sweet chocolate (melted)	

Combine the ingredients and drop by teaspoonfuls on a greased cooky sheet. Bake in a slow oven 15 minutes. Remove while they are still warm to avoid crushing.

FRUIT DROP COOKIES

1 c dark corn syrup	2 T cinnamon
1 c B. sugar	2 t cloves
1 c butter	1 t allspice
2 beaten eggs	1 c raisins

Boil the above together, stirring constantly for five minutes. When cold, add ½ t soda dissolved in 1 c sour milk, 1 c black walnuts, and enough flour to make a stiff dough. Drop by teaspoonfuls on a greased cooky sheet, and bake in a moderate oven 15 minutes.

This makes a large quantity of fruit cookies that "are different" because of the previous cooking of most of the ingredients. They will keep a long time.

FRUIT NUT BARS

2 well-beaten eggs	⅔ c chopped dates
⅔ c C. sugar	⅓ c chopped figs
½ t vanilla	⅓ c maraschino cherries
¼ t salt	(chopped)
1 t B.P.	½ c chopped nuts
	⅔ c flour

Add the sugar to the eggs and vanilla. Add the sifted-together, dry ingredients. Mix in the fruit and nuts. Spread a half inch thick on a greased cooky sheet, and bake in a slow oven 15–20 minutes. Cool and spread with an icing made of:

ICING

1 c C. sugar	2 T maraschino cherry juice
2 T thin cream or	Bits of nuts and cherries for
evaporated milk	decoration

Cut in bars and you have a good nut bar which remains white after baking.

OATMEAL COOKIES

¾ c shortening (½ lard
     and ½ butter)
1½ c sugar
3 beaten eggs
2 c flour
½ t soda
½ t B.P.

½ t salt
1 t cinnamon
1 c chopped nuts
½ c currants
1 c chopped raisins
1½ c rolled oats

Cream the shortening and sugar, and add the rest of the ingredients in the order given. Drop by teaspoonfuls one inch apart on a cooky sheet. Bake in a moderate oven 15 minutes.

These are old stand-bys that never fail. They are especially fine to take on picnics.

SAND BARS

¾ c butter
2 T G. sugar
4½ c flour

1½ c chopped pecans
C. sugar for rolling

Cream the butter and sugar; then add the flour and the nuts. Shape in two- or three-inch-long rolls with the hands, so that the marks of the four fingers will show. Bake 20 minutes on an ungreased cooky sheet in a moderate oven. Roll each cooky in C. sugar. Cool and pack the cookies away in C. sugar.

YUMMIES

½ c shortening
1 c sugar
2 well-beaten egg yolks
1 t vanilla

1½ c cake flour
1 t B.P.
½ t salt

FROSTING

2 egg whites
1 c B. sugar

1 c chopped nuts

Cream the sugar and shortening; add the egg yolks, the vanilla, and the sifted-together, dry ingredients. Spread one-fourth to one-half inch thick on a well-greased sheet cake pan. Beat the egg whites until stiff, and add the B. sugar and nuts. Blend.

Spread this frosting over the cookies and bake in a moderate oven about 25 minutes. Cool slightly and cut in squares.

These are very simple to make, and are all that their name implies.

Mrs. Harriet Belt Loveless, Columbus, Ohio.

Nut Cookies

BLACK WALNUT DROPS

1 c B. sugar	½ t nutmeg
⅔ c sour cream	1 t cinnamon
2 beaten eggs	¼ t lemon juice
½ t soda	½ c chopped nuts
2 c flour	

Mix the sugar with the cream; add the eggs and the sifted-together, dry ingredients, then the lemon juice and the nuts. Drop by teaspoonfuls on a greased, floured, cooky sheet, and bake in a moderate oven 10–12 minutes.

People who are fond of the black walnut flavor regard these as most delicious.

BUTTERNUT WAFERS

2 eggs	¼ t B.P.
1 c B. sugar	1 c chopped butternuts
⅔ c flour	

Beat the eggs well and add the sugar gradually; then add the flour, the B.P., and the nuts. Drop by teaspoonfuls on a greased cooky sheet, allowing room for spreading. Bake in a moderate oven 10–15 minutes, and remove from the pan while still warm.

"DOWN SOUTH" PECAN COOKIES

1 c butter	1 t B.P.
2 T C. sugar	2 T ice water
1 c chopped pecans	1 t vanilla
2 c flour	

Mix into a dough. Roll thin and cut in tiny round cookies. Sprinkle with sugar, and bake on a greased cooky sheet in a moderate oven 10 minutes.

These are quite "nutty."

HICKORY NUT BALLS

2 c chopped hickory nuts	1 egg
1 c sugar	⅔ c flour

Mix the beaten egg and the sugar. Add the nuts and the flour. Roll with the hand into small balls. Bake close together on a greased and floured cooky sheet in a moderate oven 12–15 minutes.

These are wonderful in flavor, and will keep well.

PEANUT BUTTER COOKIES

¾ c shortening	2 well-beaten eggs
1 c G. sugar	2 t soda in ¼ c boiling
1 c B. sugar	water
2 c peanut butter	2½ c sifted flour

Cream the shortening; add the sugars; then cream again. Add the peanut butter, and blend well. Add the eggs, and then, alternately, the flour with the water and soda mixture. Form into small balls and flatten them onto an ungreased cooky sheet with the tines of a fork, making a cross design. Bake in a moderate oven 10 minutes. These may also be shaped by a cooky press.

They are very rich, good with anything, and will keep quite well. They are a special favorite of most men.

Mrs. Dorothy Lintner Pritchard, Columbus, Ohio.

PEANUT WAFERS

1 lb. Spanish peanuts	2 T flour
1 c sugar	2 beaten eggs

Add the sugar to the eggs; then add the flour and the peanuts which have been ground with the skins. This dough, which is stiff, may be dropped or spread on a greased and floured cooky sheet. Bake in a moderate oven 20 minutes or until they begin to look slightly brown. If they are baked in a sheet, mark while still warm and remove from the pan.

These are crisp and crunchy, good alone and in combination with anything, especially a dessert with little flavor of its own—vanilla ice cream, perhaps.

Mrs. Florence Andrews, Columbus, Ohio.

Sugar Cookies
BASIC RECIPE

1 c butter	½ t salt
1 c sugar	2 t B.P.
2 eggs	1 t vanilla (or other flavor)
1 T milk	1½–2 c flour

Cream the butter; add the sugar; then cream again. Add the beaten eggs, the milk, vanilla, and one cup of flour sifted with the B.P. and the salt. Add enough additional flour to make the cookies roll easily, but use just as little as possible. Chill well. Work with a small amount at a time and keep the rest in the icebox. Cut in desired shapes, and bake on a greased cooky sheet 10 minutes.

This recipe offers the possibility of endless variation in decoration and shape. Nuts, fruit, seeds and preserves may be used as desired. Colored sugar is attractive at holiday time or in order to fit the cooky into a color scheme. Sugar cookies always have been, and probably always will be, a favorite with the young and old.

Miss Ida M. Lintner, Lyndhurst Farm, Mechanicsburg, Ohio.

BUTTERMILK COOKIES

2 c sugar	1 t soda
2 c lard	1 t nutmeg
1 egg	¼ t salt
2 c buttermilk	Flour, enough to roll

Mix the sugar and lard; add the beaten egg, the nutmeg, and salt. Add the buttermilk with the soda mixed into it. Add the flour, and roll one-fourth inch thick. Cut as desired. Bake on a greased cooky sheet in a moderate oven 10–12 minutes.

This makes a large amount, as did most of the old-time recipes which were meant for large families of hungry children and men who worked hard. This recipe has been in constant use in the Erlanbach family for three generations.

Mrs. Walter Erlanbach, New Albany, Ohio.

CARAMEL SAND TARTS

½ c shortening (½ butter and ½ lard)	1 t flavoring
1 c B. sugar	1½ c flour
1 egg	1 t B.P.
	¼ t salt

Cream the shortening and sugar. Stir in the egg and the flavoring. Add the sifted-together, dry ingredients. Chill. With the hands form bits of dough into small balls, and place on a greased cooky sheet one inch apart. Bake in a moderate oven 10 minutes.

These are delicious and crisp, and have a butterscotch flavor.

Mrs. Ada Morgan Lintner, Linthaven Farm, Powell, Ohio.

SOFT JUMBLES

½ c butter	½ t soda
1 c sugar	2½ c flour
2 eggs	1 t vanilla
½ c heavy sour cream	

Mix in the order given and drop, two inches apart, on a greased cooky sheet. Bake in a moderate oven 15 minutes.

Eat these soon after baking as they dry out quickly.

SOUR CREAM COOKIES

1 c sour cream	1 t soda
2 c sugar	1 t vanilla
1 c softened shortening	Enough flour to make a dough that will roll
2 beaten eggs	

Mix in the order given and roll one-fourth inch thick. Cut in fancy shapes and bake on a greased cooky sheet in a moderate oven 10 minutes.

Children love these made into "cooky men" or "animals," with raisins to represent eyes, and a good sprinkle of sugar to make them taste sweeter. They have been a standard cooky for generations because they are good, inexpensive, and easy to make. They will keep.   *Bertha Nafzger*, New Albany, Ohio.

SOUTHERN TEAS

1 c butter	1 t soda
2 c sugar	1 t vanilla
4 eggs	4 c flour (more if necessary)

Beat eggs and sugar together and add the softened butter. Then add the vanilla, flour, and soda. Roll thin. Cut with a small, round, or fancy cutter. Sprinkle with sugar and cinnamon, and bake on a greased cooky sheet in a moderate oven 10 minutes.

Serve with hot chocolate, or as they do in the South, with hot sassafras tea. This recipe has been handed down in the family for years and has been the "afternoon piece" of many of the children.

Mrs. Ada Morgan Lintner, Linthaven Farm, Powell, Ohio.

VANILLA WAFERS (Dropped)

⅔ c butter	⅓ c milk
⅔ c sugar	2⅓ c cake flour
2 beaten eggs	2 t B.P.
1 t vanilla	

Cream the butter and sugar; add the beaten eggs and the sifted-together, dry ingredients alternately with the milk. Add the vanilla. Drop on a greased cooky sheet, and bake in a moderate oven 10 minutes. Remove from the pan while they are still warm or they will break.

Eat while fresh as they soon dry out.

VANILLA WAFERS (Rolled)

⅓ c butter and lard (mixed)	2 c flour
1 c sugar	2 t B.P.
1 well-beaten egg	½ t salt
¼ c milk	2 t vanilla

Cream the butter and the sugar; add the rest of the ingredients in the order listed. Chill the dough for one hour. Roll thin; cut, and bake in a moderate oven about 8 minutes. If more vanilla flavor is wanted, add another teaspoonful.

This is an old favorite; good any time and with anything.

Unusual

BANANA COOKIES

¼ c butter	2 c ripe mashed bananas
1 c sugar	1½ c flour
2 beaten eggs	1 t soda
½ t salt	1½ c chopped black walnuts

Cream the butter and sugar, add the eggs, bananas, and then the sifted-together, dry ingredients to which the nuts have been added. Drop on a greased cooky sheet, and bake in a slow oven 20–25 minutes.

These are moist and rich, and should be used soon after baking.

Mrs. Genevieve Forsyth, Alexandria, Ohio.

DIXIE SQUARES

½ c clear chicken fat	2 t B.P.
1½ c sugar	¼ t salt
2 well-beaten eggs	2 squares chocolate
¼ c spiced pear juice	½ c chopped nut meats
¼ c orange juice	½ c chopped raisins
1½ c pastry flour	⅔ c hot, mashed sweet
½ t each cloves, allspice, cinnamon	potatoes

Mix the fat and sugar. Add the potato, egg, pear, and orange juice. Add the sifted-together, dry ingredients, then the melted chocolate, the nuts, and raisins. Spread one-fourth inch thick on a greased tin, and bake 15–20 minutes in a moderate oven. Dust with C. sugar and cut in two-inch squares.

These are excellent. Any fat may be substituted for the chicken fat, but that is especially good.

"GUMDROPS"

2 eggs
1 c B. sugar
1 c flour
f.g..salt
½ t cinnamon

¼ c chopped nuts
½ c shredded gumdrops
(omit any flavors that are
not desired)

Beat the eggs well and add the sugar, then beat again. Add the nuts and gumdrops to the sifted-together, dry ingredients. Drop on a greased cooky sheet, and bake in a moderate oven 20 minutes.

These are unusual in flavor, and should be used at once as they do not keep well.

HAWAIIAN COOKIES

1 egg
⅓ c sugar
¼ c chopped nuts
¼ c crushed pineapple
½ c flour

¼ c fine cake crumbs
(graham cracker or cereal
very finely crushed)
¼ t salt
1 t B.P.

Beat the egg; add the sugar, pineapple, drained very dry, crumbs, the sifted-together, dry ingredients, and the nuts. Drop on a greased and floured cooky sheet, and bake in a moderate oven 10 minutes. Dust with C. sugar.

These are moist when first made, but become crisp upon standing. They do not keep long.

HUCKLEBERRY DROPS

⅓ c shortening
1 c sugar
2 egg yolks
¼ c milk
1 T lemon juice

½ lemon rind, grated
1 c canned, drained,
huckleberries
2 c flour
2 t B.P.

Mix the shortening and sugar; add the egg yolks, the lemon rind and juice, the berries, and the milk alternately with the sifted-together, dry ingredients. Drop on a greased cooky sheet, and bake in a moderate oven 10–15 minutes.

Use as soon as baked as they do not stay fresh long.

AUSTRIA

LINZER COOKIES
CHOCOLATE SQUARES

For rich, flavorful, good cookies, try these. They are richer than the German, as attractive as the French, lighter than the Italian, as nutty and fruity as the American, and certainly much more full of jam and preserves than any of them. You'll have to spend a good bit of time decorating and glazing, but the results will be worth it. Good they are, and so tempting that you would give up a reducing diet to enjoy their excellence.

BRANDY DROPS

2 egg yolks	1 T brandy (or heavy
3 T sugar	fruit juice)
1 T bread crumbs	1 c ground hazelnuts
	1 egg white

Stir the egg yolks with the sugar until foamy. Add the bread crumbs moistened with the brandy. Then add the nuts and the lightly beaten egg white. Drop by teaspoonfuls on a greased cooky sheet, and bake in a moderate oven 10–15 minutes.

These have an unusual flavor if the brandy is used.

CHOCOLATE BALLS

2 T butter	1 square chocolate
½ c sugar	⅔ c nuts
2 egg yolks	⅔ c flour

Cream the butter and sugar; add the egg yolks and beat. Then add the melted chocolate, flour, and nuts. Make into little balls on a greased cooky sheet, and bake in a moderate oven 10 minutes. But watch to prevent burning.

CHOCOLATE VIENNA COOKIES

¾ c butter	2 squares chocolate
1 c sugar	1½ c flour
5 eggs	3 t B.P.

Cream the butter and sugar and add the beaten egg yolks. Add the sifted-together, dry ingredients, the melted chocolate, and fold in the beaten egg whites. Fill small, greased muffin tins two thirds full of the batter. Bake in a moderate oven 15 minutes. Split and fill with apricot jam. Sprinkle with C. sugar.

CHOCOLATE VIENNA
COOKIES FILLED WITH JAM

DATE BITS

3 egg whites	1 c almond slices,
1 c sugar	unblanched
	1 c dates, sliced lengthwise

Stir the sugar gradually into the stiffly beaten egg whites. Add the dates and almonds. Drop by teaspoonfuls on a greased, floured, cooky sheet, two inches apart. Bake in a moderate oven 10 minutes.

They spread wide like a large, flat macaroon. This mixture may be spread on saltines and baked in the same manner and an entirely different effect will result—more like the American *Marguerite*.

HAZELNUT SLICES

1 c ground hazelnuts   Stiff raspberry or
1/3 c sugar   strawberry jam
1 unbeaten egg white

Mix all but the jam. Form into a long strip two inches wide.
Make a depression the length of the strip and fill it with the jam.
Bake on a greased pan in a moderate oven 15–20 minutes. Remove from the oven; cool; cut in half-inch slices, and remove
from the pan.

This is an unusual looking cooky with an equally unusual flavor
resulting from the jam, nut combination. It is best served with
coffee or a cold beverage.

JELLY ROUNDS

1/2 c butter   1/4 c ground nuts
1 c flour   1 t lemon juice
1/4 c sugar   1 lemon rind, grated

Mix in the order given. Chill 20 minutes. Roll one-fourth
inch thick and cut in rounds. Bake on a greased cooky sheet in
a moderate oven 10 minutes. Immediately before serving decorate the center of each cooky with a spot of tart jam or jelly and
sprinkle with C. sugar.

Use very soon after baking, as they do not keep well.

LINZER COOKIES

1 c shortening   1 lemon rind, grated
1 c sugar   2 c flour
2 egg yolks   1 t cinnamon
1 c ground, unblanched   1/2 t cloves
  almonds   Raspberry jam

Cream the shortening and sugar until light and fluffy. Add
the egg yolks, almonds, lemon rind, and then the dry ingredients sifted together. Roll to one-fourth inch thickness. Cut in
rounds. Decorate with a spot of jam, or spread the entire cooky
with jam, and cover the top with strips of dough placed in criss-

cross fashion. Bake on an ungreased cooky sheet in a moderate oven 10–15 minutes.

This is a very rich cooky, but fine with coffee or a tart, cold beverage. Never serve it with a rich dessert.

NUT COOKIES

⅔ c sugar	½ c ground, blanched
1 egg	almonds
	¼ c flour

Make a dough. Roll one-half inch thick. Cut in strips. Brush with egg white and sprinkle with sugar. Bake on a greased cooky sheet in a moderate oven 10 minutes.

ORANGE CREAM DROPS

¼ c sugar	½ c chopped, candied
½ c very heavy, thick	orange peel
cream	⅓ c flour
½ c chopped, blanched	⅛ t soda (if sour cream
almonds	is used)

Mix the cream and sugar together; add the rest of the ingredients. Drop by teaspoonfuls, one inch apart, on a greased cooky sheet. Bake in a moderate oven 10 minutes.

SACHER STRIPS

¼ c butter	1 c ground, unblanched
⅔ c sugar	almonds
1½ squares melted	4 egg yolks
chocolate	4 egg whites
	½ c flour

Melt the butter; add the chocolate and the sugar. Add the almonds and stir well. Mix in the egg yolks, then the flour, and last fold in the stiffly beaten egg whites. Spread one-half inch thick on a greased cooky sheet, and bake in a moderate oven 15 minutes. Cool slightly; cut in bars; sprinkle with C. sugar and serve.

For a less expensive, though very good, product, use ground coconut instead of the almonds. But for a real Austrian cooky, you must use the almonds.

SOUR CREAM JAM COOKIES

⅓ c shortening	f.g. salt
⅓ c sugar	1½ c flour
1 c sour cream	¼ t soda
6 egg yolks	1 c jam

Cream the shortening and sugar; add the sour cream, egg yolks, and salt. Add the flour sifted with the soda. Fill greased muffin pan half full of the mixture, and bake in a moderate oven about 15 minutes. Break while still warm; spread with jam and press the layers together again. Sprinkle with C. sugar and serve at once.

These, with coffee, are very good, served as a dessert. They are also excellent for "winter afternoon" coffee.

VANILLA CRESCENTS

1 c butter	1 vanilla bean (or 2 t
5 T sugar	vanilla; but for best flavor,
2 c flour	use the bean)
1 c ground, blanched almonds	

Mix the first three as for pie dough. Grind the other two and add to the first mixture. With the hands form small crescents or, if you prefer, roll the dough and cut out crescents. Bake on an ungreased cooky sheet in a hot oven 8–10 minutes. Dip while still warm in C. sugar moistened with vanilla.

VIENNESE KISSES

2 egg whites	⅔ c ground nuts
f.g. salt	¼ t vanilla
⅔ c sugar	

Add the salt and sugar to the egg whites and beat over hot water until the mixture will hold its shape. Add the nuts and the vanilla. Drop by teaspoonfuls on a greased, floured, cooky sheet, and bake in a slow oven until light brown. Remove from the pan at once.

VIENNESE COCONUT MACAROONS

⅓ c butter	2 t heavy cream
½ c sugar	½ t vanilla
2 eggs	⅓ c flour
1 c coconut	4 T cornstarch
6 crushed vanilla wafers	½ t B.P.

Cream the butter and sugar; add the well-beaten eggs, cream, and vanilla. Sift the dry ingredients, and add to the first mixture. Add the coconut and the wafers. Drop by teaspoonfuls, one inch apart, on a greased cooky sheet, and bake in a moderate oven until brown on top.

VIENNESE PORCUPINE SQUARES

4 eggs	½ t lemon juice
⅞ c sugar	1 orange rind, grated
⅞ c flour	Chocolate filling and icing
1 t B.P.	Almond slivers
⅛ t salt	

Beat the eggs until they are light, then gradually add the sugar. Fold in the sifted-together, dry ingredients, and add the flavorings. Spread on a cooky sheet lined with wax paper, and bake in a hot oven 10–12 minutes. Remove the paper and cut the cookies in two-inch squares. Put two together with chocolate filling; ice the outside with chocolate icing; stick almond slivers all over the square to represent the porcupine quills.

CHOCOLATE FILLING

Melt 1½ squares of unsweetened chocolate over hot water, and add ⅔ c condensed milk. Stir until thick and add ½ t vanilla. Cool slightly before using.

Chocolate Icing

1½ c C. sugar	1½ t butter
3 t cocoa	½ t vanilla

Put the butter in a bowl and add the sifted C. sugar and cocoa. Add enough hot water to make a creamy icing of proper spreading consistency. Add vanilla.

VIENNESE SANDWICH COOKIES

1 c butter	½ c milk
1½ c sugar	3 t B.P.
3 eggs	4 c flour

Cream the butter and sugar; add the beaten eggs and the milk; then beat well. Add the sifted-together, dry ingredients, and work into a soft dough. Divide into two parts. Press each part on a greased, square cake pan, and bake in a hot oven about 10 minutes. Cool. Spread one layer with prune jam and place the other layer on top. Cut in squares or strips and sprinkle with C. sugar.

Serve at once. They do not keep.

Prune Jam

1 lb. prunes (2⅔ c)	⅔ c sugar
2 T lemon juice	1 T powdered cardamon

Wash the prunes. Simmer till well done. Stone, chop, add the other ingredients, and simmer 5 minutes.

VIENNA WAFERS

¾ c butter	1 t B.P.
½ c sugar	1 egg
2 T lemon juice	¼ c nut meats
1½ c flour	

Cream the butter and sugar; then add the unbeaten egg, lemon juice, flour, and B.P. Roll thin; cut; place a nut meat in the center of each cooky, and bake on a greased cooky sheet in a moderate oven 10 minutes.

ENGLAND

There has been a tendency on the part of many Americans who have been in England to say uncomplimentary things about English cookery. In some cases this may have been justified.

However, if an Englishman were to come to America and eat all his meals in restaurants and hotels, he might also have something true and yet quite untrue to say of "characteristic American food." Be that as it may, even the person who most berates the over-cooked vegetables and the rhubarb with custard sauce dessert, has only praise for the grand things that go along with an English tea. He can't forget the *Sultana Cakes,* the *Sand Tarts,* those very special *Jam Cakes,* and the unusual flavor of rose water. He likes the things that he might call cookies

SAND TARTS
JUMBLES (ROLLED)
JUMBLES (PLAIN)
ORANGE WELLS

and that the Englishman calls "crackers" or "biscuits." He wishes he might taste again and again some of those "chewy ginger things." Most of the English cookies taste more like the "things that mother used to make" than do the cookies of other countries, not excepting Germany.

Many of these recipes come from the Morgan and Reece families, who came to America from Herefordshire, England, and fortunately remembered to bring along the family cookery secrets. Some came from family friends who preserved the good, old custom of serving a few good cookies along with the bread-and-butter teas.

English cookies will be liked by most people. They have an added advantage of being easy to make, and afford opportunity for endless variety. The *Sand Tarts* may be decorated, and the jam in the *Jam Cakes* may be varied. The extra things that go into the tea crackers may be so different each time that it will seem as if a brand new cooky has been made.

ABERGAVENNY NUTS

1 c Orleans molasses (warm)	1 t salt
1 c sugar	1 T ginger
1 c shortening (½ butter	2 t soda
and ½ lard)	½ c warm water

Mix all in the order given. Add enough flour to form a stiff dough. Mold with the hands into small balls. Press into the top of each ball a strip of preserved ginger. Bake on a greased cooky sheet, one inch apart, in a moderate oven 10–15 minutes.

This is a very old recipe named after the Morgan farm in Herefordshire, England.

AFTERNOON TEA STRIPS

1 c sugar	1 t B.P.
½ c butter	1½ c flour
4 eggs	½ t vanilla
⅛ t salt	

Cream the sugar and butter together; add the unbeaten eggs one at a time. Beat well. Stir in the dry ingredients (except the B.P.) and the vanilla. Beat 20 minutes and then add the B.P. Bake in a thin sheet on a greased cooky sheet, in a moderate oven 10 minutes. When slightly brown, remove from the oven and cool. Cut in strips; dust with C. sugar and serve.

These are "tea time" favorites, and should be used soon after baking as they do not keep well.

Mrs. H. Hanson, Kirkwood, Missouri.

BETSEY PANTLE'S COCONUT DROPS

1 c sugar	2 egg whites
2 c coconut	Juice of ½ lemon

Beat the egg whites, lemon, and sugar until the mass will hold its shape. Stir in the coconut. Drop by teaspoonfuls on a greased, floured, cooky sheet, an inch apart. Bake in a slow oven 15 minutes, but watch to prevent burning.

These are like macaroons and, if packed in tin, will keep well.

COFFEE RAISIN DROPS

1 c G. sugar	½ c raisin juice
1 c B. sugar	½ c coffee
1 c shortening	5 c flour
2 eggs	1 t B.P.
1 c cooked raisins	⅔ t soda
½ t nutmeg	⅛ t salt
½ t cinnamon	

Cook 1 c seeded or seedless raisins in 1 c water about five minutes in order to get the raisin juice. Cream the shortening, and add the sugars, and cream again. Add the unbeaten eggs, and beat well.

Add the coffee and the raisin juice, then the sifted-together, dry ingredients. Add the raisins. Drop, one inch apart, on a greased cooky sheet, and bake in a moderate oven about 15 minutes.

This amount makes a large number of cookies. Half the recipe is quite enough for an average family.

Mrs. Elizabeth Esson Schoenberger, Wharton, Ohio.

DATE SCONES

⅓ c butter	⅔ c chopped dates
⅓ c sugar	1 egg
3 c flour	½ c milk

Mix the sugar, flour, and dates; add the milk, beaten egg and melted butter. Pat the dough thin on a greased cooky sheet. Bake in a quick oven 8–10 minutes. When cool, mark in squares.

These are like a date cracker—excellent with tea.

Mrs. H. Hanson, Kirkwood, Missouri.

DROP COOKIES

(1)

½ c shortening	½ t soda
½ c sugar	2 c flour
½ c sour milk	

(2)

¼ t each, cloves, cinnamon	⅔ c raisins
⅓ c currants	2 T cider

Add 1 to 2. Mix. Drop on a greased cooky sheet and bake in a moderate oven 15 minutes. All raisins may be used in place of the currants. 1 T lemon juice and 1 T water may be used in place of the cider.

EFFIE'S CAKES

2 c shortening	1 T mixed spice
1 c sugar	2 T rose water (any fruit
3 egg yolks	juice or plain water if the
2 egg whites	rose flavor is not liked)
1 c currants	3 c flour
½ t soda	

Cream the shortening and add the sugar, beaten eggs, and rose water. Add the sifted-together, dry ingredients, and the currants. Mix well. Drop on a greased cooky sheet, and bake in a moderate oven 12–15 minutes.

This is an old-time recipe and makes a huge quantity.

Mrs. Ada Morgan Lintner, Linthaven Farm, Powell, Ohio.

ELIZABETH BLANTON'S CURRANT COOKIES

½ c butter	½ c currants
4 T sugar	2 T water if necessary in
2 c flour	mixing

Mix in order with hands. Roll; cut and glaze with egg yolk and sugar. Bake on a greased cooky sheet in a moderate oven 10-15 minutes.

FAIRY CAKES

½ c butter	⅓ c candied cherries
½ c sugar	(or maraschino)
3 eggs	1½ c flour
1 T lemon juice	1½ t B.P.

Cream the butter and sugar, and add the beaten egg yolks and lemon juice. Add the sifted-together, dry ingredients to which the chopped cherries have been added. Fold in the stiffly beaten egg whites, and bake in small, greased, gem pans 20 minutes in a moderately slow oven. Decorate the top of each cake with a piece of cherry, before baking, if desired.

Use soon after they are baked, as they dry out and lose their "fairy" quality.

FRUIT WAFERS

¼ c butter	½ t cloves
¼ c sugar	2 eggs
¼ c raisins	2 t strong rose water
¼ c currants	(substitute any fruit juice)
½ t cinnamon	1⅓ c flour

Cream the butter and sugar; add the ground fruit, the spice, the flour, the beaten eggs, and the rose water. Roll thin; cut, and bake on a greased cooky sheet in a moderate oven 8–10 minutes. Watch to prevent burning.

These will keep well several days.

JAM COOKIES

2 T butter	¼ t salt
4 T sugar	1 t B.P.
1½ c flour	Jam
2 eggs	

Cream the butter and sugar. Add the egg yolks which have been beaten one minute. Add the sifted-together, dry ingredients, and finally fold in the stiffly beaten egg whites. Pour on a greased, square, cake pan, one-half inch thick, and bake in a moderate oven 20 minutes. When almost cold, split the cake; put it together with your favorite stiff jam, then cut in strips, and sprinkle with C. sugar and serve.

These must not be kept more than one day as the jam soaks, but if you cannot use them as soon as baked, do not put the jam in until you are ready to use them. They are especially fine for tea.

JUMBLES

1 c sugar	2 c flour
⅓ c butter	1 lemon rind, grated
1 c dark corn syrup	½ t ginger
2 eggs	

Cream the sugar and butter; add the corn syrup and beaten eggs. Add the rest in order given. Drop two inches apart on a well-greased cooky sheet (this is very important because they will run), and bake in a moderate oven 8-10 minutes. They may be shaped in cones as they come from the oven. If they become too brittle to shape, return them to the oven for a minute to start again. If you do not want to shape them, decorate the center of each with a nut and bake them as large, thin, flat jumbles.

These are favorites with those who prize chewiness in cookies.

LEMON CRACKERS

2½ c sugar
1 c lard
2 c milk
¼ t salt
"Five cents worth" of
lemon oil (½ t)

"Five cents worth" of car-
bonate of ammonia (1½ t)
Flour (about 8 c)
2 eggs

Mix in the order given, adding flour until the dough is stiff enough to roll. Roll thin; cut in squares; prick with a fork— as for crackers; bake on a greased cooky sheet 10 minutes.

These have a very distinctive flavor not at all like the usual lemon juice and rind cooky. They save well, and are a favorite with those who cultivate the taste for unique flavor. This recipe has been used in the Morgan family for many years.

Mrs. Ada Morgan Lintner, Linthaven Farm, Powell, Ohio.

LONDON STRIPS

½ c butter
¼ c C. sugar
⅛ t salt
2 egg yolks

1 c flour
⅓ c chopped nuts
¾ c jam

Mix in the order given. Spread thin on a greased, square pan, and bake in a moderate oven 10 minutes. Spread with jam and cover with *Topping*.

TOPPING

4 egg whites
¼ c shredded almond

¼ c C. sugar
½ t vanilla

Beat the egg whites until stiff. Add the sugar and vanilla, and beat again. Sprinkle the strips with almonds, and bake in a slow oven 15 minutes. Cool and cut in squares.

These are sweet and rich, and excellent if used the same day as made.

MORGAN GINGER CHEWS

¾ c Orleans molasses	¼ t B.P.
2 T butter	1 t ginger
2 c flour	f.g. salt

Boil the molasses 1 minute. Add the butter and the rest of the ingredients. Work into a dough. Form into rolls and chill from one hour to all night. Cut in thin slices, and bake on a greased cooky sheet 10 minutes in a moderately hot oven.

These are perfectly described by the name. Very good to munch on while reading.

Mrs. Ada Morgan Lintner, Linthaven Farm, Powell, Ohio.

OLD-TIMER'S COOKIES

½ c butter or lard	⅛ t salt
⅓ c sugar	½ t soda
2 c flour	1 beaten egg
1½ t B.P.	½ t vanilla

With hands rub the butter into the flour, then add the remaining ingredients. Roll thin; cut in fancy shapes; bake on a greased cooky sheet in a hot oven 10 minutes. Watch to prevent burning.

This is a very old recipe which was obtained from a woman, now seventy-nine years old, who remembers that it was used in her home when she was a girl and that she was told it was used in her mother's home when she was young.

Mrs. H. Hanson, Kirkwood, Missouri.

ORANGE GINGER NUTS

½ c butter	½ t B.P.
1 c sugar	2½ t ginger
1 egg	⅓ c candied peel
2 c flour	

Cream the butter and sugar. Add the unbeaten egg. Beat well. Add the sifted-together, dry ingredients along with the peel. Shape into balls of the size of a hickory nut, and bake on a greased cooky sheet, one inch apart, in a hot oven about 10 minutes. Watch to prevent burning.

These have a flavor much different from the usual ginger cooky.

ORANGE WELLS

¾ c shortening	¼ t nutmeg
2 c sugar	1 t vanilla
¼ c milk	3 t B.P.
2 eggs (beaten)	4 c flour

Cream the shortening and sugar; add the milk, eggs, vanilla. Add 3 c of flour with the other dry ingredients, then add enough additional flour to make a dough which will roll. Roll thin; cut in rounds. Place a small spoonful of orange marmalade in the center of each cooky. Fold the edges around this to form a tricorn. Press lightly to make them hold their shape. Bake on a greased cooky sheet in a moderate oven 10–12 minutes. Be sure the marmalade is stiff, and plan to use these soon after baking as they do not save well.

PARKIN DROPS

1 c rolled oats	½ c flour
½ c dark corn syrup	½ t ginger
2 T butter	2 T milk
3 T sugar	½ t B.P.

Warm the syrup. Add the butter, the oats, the sugar, and the ginger. Remove from the fire. Cool. Then add the flour, sifted with the B.P., and the milk. Drop by teaspoonfuls on a greased cooky sheet, and bake in a moderately slow oven 20 minutes.

These are flat, wonderfully chewy, and have a strange flavor.

PARKIN STRIPS

¼ c lard	1 t ginger
½ c Orleans molasses	½ t soda
½ c sugar	1 t B.P.
1 egg	⅛ t salt
2 c flour	¾ c sour milk

Warm the lard and molasses together. Add the sugar and the egg; then the sifted-together, dry ingredients alternately with the milk. Spread thin on a greased, square cake pan. Bake in a moderate oven 15 minutes. Remove and cool. Ice with lemon glaze. Cut in long, finger-like strips.

These are good, not too rich, and fine with tea. This is a very good old English recipe.

Mrs. H. Hanson, Kirkwood, Missouri.

SAND TARTS

2 egg (reserving 1 white)	1 c softened butter
2 c sugar	3 c flour

Mix in the order given. Roll thin and cut in rounds. Brush with unbeaten egg white; sprinkle with sugar and cinnamon. Press a nut or raisin on the top of each tart, and bake in a hot oven 10 minutes. Ice-box method may be used. (p. 22)

This has been used in the Morgan family for at least three generations. Sand Tarts are well liked as a crisp cooky. They are characteristically English.

SHREWSBURY SEED CAKES

1 c butter	2 c flour
¾ c sugar	1 egg

Mix the butter into the flour, then add the rest of the ingredients. Roll thin and cut in fancy shapes. Sprinkle with caraway or anise seeds, and bake on a greased cooky sheet in a hot oven 5 minutes.

SULTANA DROPS

½ c butter	1 c chopped nuts
½ c sugar	2 T chopped citron
2 eggs	2 c flour
½ c raisins	1 t B.P.
1 orange rind, grated	

Cream the butter and sugar. Add the slightly beaten eggs, then the flour along with the B.P. and the fruit. Mix well. Drop by teaspoonfuls on a greased cooky sheet, and bake in a moderate oven 10–15 minutes.

These should not be eaten the same day as made. They keep well.

TEA CRACKERS

¼ c butter	1 egg
¼ c sugar	f.g. salt
½ c flour	½ t flavor

Cream the butter; add the sugar, and cream again. Add the flavor, the well-beaten egg, the salt, and the flour. Drop by teaspoonfuls on a greased cooky sheet, and bake in a moderate oven 13–15 minutes. Do not let them get too brown. Nuts, currants, raisins, peel, or pieces of dried fruit may be used for decoration.

These are fine for tea—not so rich as to destroy the dinner appetite.

YORKSHIRE ROCKS

½ c butter	¼ t salt
2 c flour	3 T candied orange peel
½ c ground raisins	1 egg
1 t B.P.	1 T water

Mix a stiff dough. Form into small balls, and bake on a greased cooky sheet in a moderate oven 15 minutes. Roll in C. sugar while still warm.

These should be used soon after they are made. They are good with tea or coffee.

YORKSHIRE TEA CAKES

¾ c shortening	1¼ c flour
1 c sugar	1 c currants
4 eggs	

Cream the shortening and sugar. Add all the eggs and beat hard one minute. Blend in the flour and currants. Spread ½ inch thick on a shallow greased pan and bake in a moderate oven 30 minutes. Cut into squares while slightly warm.

FRANCE

NUT MERINGUES
BASIC PETITS FOURS

Culinary France is synonymous with good food. In the matter of cookies we think at once of French pastry and the *Petits Fours* which have an international reputation. French people like "fancy things"—things that obviously consume much time and effort in the making, though the money expended is usually slight.

The pastry itself costs little, but the individual can decide just how much is to go on and in the cooky for decoration. If the taste is extravagant, the product will be costly, for fruit and nuts soon run up the grocery bill. However, it may be worth it.

Meringues and kisses, puffy things which have a wonderful flavor and delight both the eyes and the stomach, seem difficult to make when one considers all the beating and care re-

74

quired to insure just the proper baking. But once the art is practiced, it is soon mastered. Whatever extra effort is needed is justified, for the pleasure exhibited by the ultimate consumer of the *gâteau* will inspire the culinary artist to perform another, perhaps more difficult, feat.

APRICOT TEA CAKES

Line small, greased muffin tins with *Basic Petits Fours* recipe. Place in the center of each an apricot which has been soaked in cooking sherry or fruit juice 30 minutes. Sprinkle with C. sugar and finely chopped nuts. Pull the dough close around the apricot like a tart. Bake in a moderate oven 20 minutes.

These are fine, but will keep only a day or so.

BASIC PETITS FOURS

½ c butter	½ t B.P.
½ c sugar	½ t vanilla
2 eggs	2 c flour

Mix the butter, sugar, eggs, and vanilla. Add the sifted-together, dry ingredients and mix. Chill. Roll thin. Cut in fancy shapes, and decorate with colored sugar, candied fruit, nuts, coconut, jelly, etc. Bake on a greased cooky sheet in a moderate oven 15 minutes.

It is well to use only half the dough in this recipe, saving the other half for the *Apricot Tea Cakes.*

BERNADINS

To the recipe for *Pain d'Amand,* on page 82, add 2 c shelled, blanched, ground almonds. Follow the same method, but glaze each slice with egg white and sprinkle with G. sugar before baking.

These are very attractive because of the glazed surface, and very tasty because of the ground almonds.

Mme. Alcide Brasseur, Lancaster, Ohio.

COCOA-NUT DROPS

1 c blanched, chopped almonds	2 egg whites
1 T water	1 square melted chocolate
1 c C. sugar	½ c flour

Mix the almonds, water, and the sugar. Add the melted chocolate, the flour, and the egg whites. Drop on a greased cooky sheet, and let them dry 20 minutes. Bake in a moderate oven 15 minutes. Remove from the pan while they are still warm, being careful not to crush.

COFFEE KISSES

¼ c strong, clear coffee	3 egg whites
1¼ c sugar	3 T C. sugar

Boil the coffee and sugar to the "soft ball" stage. Pour on the stiffly beaten egg whites, gradually beating all the time. Stir in the C. sugar. Drop on a greased and floured cooky sheet. Sprinkle the top of each kiss with a little pulverized or very finely ground coffee, and bake in a very slow oven until brown. Remove carefully!

CHOCOLATE PEAKS

2 squares chocolate	2⅔ c blanched almond strips
⅔ c sugar	3 egg whites
½ t vanilla	f.g. salt

Melt the chocolate over water. Heat the almonds in the oven. Add the sugar to the chocolate. Add the egg whites one at a time, beating well after each addition. Add the toasted almonds, the salt, and the vanilla. Drop in small peaks on a greased cooky sheet, and dry one hour. Then bake in a moderate oven 10–12 minutes. Watch to prevent burning.

These are like baked fudge, rich and delicious.

CREAM CAKES

3 eggs	1 t B.P.
1 c sugar	1½ t lemon juice
1½ c cake flour	¼ t salt
2 T cold water	

Beat the eggs until light, and add, gradually, the sugar, the cold water, and the lemon juice. Sift the dry ingredients twice, and fold into the mixture. Spread one-half inch thick on a square pan lined with wax paper. Bake in a slow oven 20–30 minutes. When cool, divide the layer in half and put together, sandwich fashion, with the filling. Sprinkle with C. sugar, and cut in squares.

FILLING

2½ c milk
  2 T cornstarch
  2 eggs

1 c sugar
½ c butter
1 t vanilla

Mix the sugar and cornstarch, then add the cold milk. Cook until thick, and pour slowly on the beaten eggs. Stir in the butter and vanilla, and mix well.

FRENCH ALMOND MACAROONS

½ lb. almond paste
1 c sugar
3 egg whites

2 T pastry flour
½ c C. sugar
⅛ t salt

Mix the paste well; add sugar slowly; then egg whites. Blend. Add sifted-together dry ingredients. Shape with pastry tube or spoon on a well-greased cooky sheet. Let stand 1 to 8 hours. Brush lightly with cold water. Bake 30 minutes in a slow oven. They may be decorated with fruit and nuts before baking, or frosted afterward. This is the traditional almond macaroon.

FRENCH PASTRY No. 1

½ c butter
1 c sugar
½ c milk
2 egg whites

1½ t B.P.
1⅔ c flour
1 t flavoring

Cream the butter and the sugar; add the milk, the flavor, and the sifted-together, dry ingredients. Fold in the stiffly beaten egg whites. Spread one inch thick on a greased cake pan, and bake in a moderate oven 20–30 minutes or until it springs back when touched with the finger. Cool. Cut in fancy shapes. Frost and decorate as desired.

These are rich, light, and delicious but will not keep long.

FRENCH PASTRY No. 2

2 c sugar	2 t B.P.
¾ c butter (1½ sticks)	3 c cake flour
1¼ c milk	1 t vanilla
6 egg whites	

Cream the butter, add the sugar gradually, and cream again. Add the sifted-together, dry ingredients alternately with the milk. Add the vanilla. Fold in the stiffly beaten egg whites. Bake in a sheet, one inch thick, on a cake pan lined with waxed paper, in a moderate oven 30 minutes. Remove the waxed paper. Cool. Cut in fancy shapes, and decorate as desired.

Mrs. Alvin Zurcher, Chillicothe, Ohio.

FRENCH PASTRY No. 3

4 egg whites	½ lemon rind, grated
4 egg yolks	1½ t cornstarch
1 c sugar	1½ t B.P.
3 T cold water	¼ t salt
½ t vanilla	2 c cake flour
1 t lemon juice	

Beat the egg whites until stiff and dry; add one half of the sugar, and set aside. Then beat the yolks till lemon colored, and add the other half of the sugar, the water, lemon juice and rind, and vanilla. Combine the two mixtures by pouring one into the other *slowly.* Sift in the dry ingredients which have been sifted three times. *Do not beat!* Spread the mixture, one inch thick, on the wax-paper-lined cake tin. Bake in a slow oven 30–40 minutes. Remove the waxed paper. Cool. Cut in fancy shapes, and frost with *Fluffy Frosting,* or decorate as you wish.

FRENCH TRIANGLES

½ c butter	½ t soda
1 c sugar	⅜ c sour milk
1 egg	3 c flour
1 orange rind, grated	

Cream the butter and sugar; add the unbeaten egg and the orange rind. Beat for one minute. Add the soda dissolved in the milk. Then add the flour. Chill one-half hour. Work with only one third of the dough at a time, leaving the rest in the icebox to chill. (The colder it is, the easier it will be to work with, less flour will be needed in rolling, and the cooky will be finer and crispier.) Roll thin, cut in triangles, brush with egg white, and sprinkle with chopped nuts. Bake in a moderate oven on a greased cooky sheet 8–10 minutes.

HAZELNUT STICKS

DOUGH

1 egg white	¾ c ground hazelnuts
¾ c C. sugar	

TOPPING

1 egg yolk	½ t vanilla
6 T C. sugar	

Beat the egg white, then add the sugar and nuts. Pat to one-half inch thickness on a board sprinkled with C. sugar. Put on the topping. Let stand on the board 10 minutes. Cut in strips. Place on a greased, floured, cooky sheet, and let dry 10 minutes more. Bake in a slow oven until a golden brown color. Remove at once, being careful not to crush.

These are excellent, and they keep well.

HONEY STRIPS

½ c shortening	3½–4 c flour
⅓ c sugar	¼ t salt
1 egg	2 t B.P.
1 c warmed honey	⅔ c blanched, chopped
2 T lemon juice	almonds

Mix the sugar and the shortening. Add the unbeaten egg, and beat well. Add the honey, lemon juice, and the sifted-together, dry ingredients. Last of all, add the nuts. Roll thin; cut in strips, and bake on a greased cooky sheet in a moderate oven 10–12 minutes.

JUMBLES

1 c sugar	½ lemon rind, grated
½ c butter	½ t soda
⅓ c milk	1 t nutmeg
1⅔ c flour	1 T brandy, wine, or
1 egg	fruit juice
⅓ c raisins	

Cream the butter, sugar, and add the egg, nutmeg, wine, and lemon rind. Beat well. Add the milk, and the raisins which have been added to the sifted-together, dry ingredients. Drop on a greased cooky sheet, two inches apart, and bake in a moderate oven 10–12 minutes.

The brandy gives these a wonderful flavor.

LITTLE FRENCH MERINGUES

2 egg whites	f.g. salt
⅓ c C. sugar	6 drops of flavoring

Beat the egg whites and salt until they hold their shape. Slowly add the sugar which has been sifted once. Continue to beat as the sugar is added. Add the flavoring. Drop from the tip of a teaspoon on a dampened paper fastened to a board about one inch thick (a bread board is good). Make the meringue about one and one-half inches in diameter. Sprinkle with C. sugar or coconut, and bake in a slow oven from 45–60 minutes. Then increase the heat and let them brown slightly. They are done when they can be easily lifted from the paper. Remove carefully.

These, being very small, will be cooked throughout and will have none of the soft, spongy part sometimes found in large meringues.

They may be colored with vegetable coloring before being baked, or nuts may be used in place of the coconut.

NUT WAFERS

½ c chopped, blanched almonds	1 c C. sugar
1 T water	2 egg whites
	½ t vanilla

Add the water to the almonds and sugar. Set over a fire to dry; stir often as this mixture burns easily. When very stiff and dry, add the unbeaten egg whites and beat the mixture to a medium-soft paste. Drop on a greased cooky sheet two inches apart. Let them dry three hours before baking. Bake in a moderate oven 10 minutes. One square of chocolate may be added for chocolate nut wafers.

This is a typical French recipe. It takes a great deal of care to make it just right, but the result is worth the labor for those who care for the fragile, sweet, confection-like cooky. They keep well in a covered tin.

NUT MERINGUES

2 egg whites	¾ c chopped nuts
⅔ c C. sugar	½ t vanilla
f.g. salt	

Mix the sugar and the nuts. Beat the egg whites, and salt until stiff and dry. Add the vanilla, and mix in the sugar-nut mixture. Drop on a greased cooky sheet, and bake about 20 minutes, until brown, in a moderate oven.

Almonds should be used for the real French flavor. These are fine, but should be used the same day as made.

ORANGE MACAROONS

1 c ground, blanched almonds	3 egg whites
⅔ c sifted C. sugar	f.g. salt
¼ c flour	1 orange rind, grated

Sift the flour and sugar. Add the nuts and orange rind. Add the salt to the egg whites and beat until they are stiff and dry. Gently fold in the first mixture. Drop on a greased cooky sheet, and bake in a slow oven 20 minutes. Remove carefully.

PAIN D'AMANDS

1 c butter	1 t almond flavoring
1 c B. sugar	½ t cinnamon
1 c G. sugar	1 t soda
2 eggs (3, if small)	4 c flour
2 T honey	

Cream the butter; add the sugars, and cream again. Add the eggs and blend well. Add the honey and the flavoring. Then add the sifted-together, dry ingredients. Form into long rolls; wrap in waxed paper (icebox molds may be used) and chill at least four hours. Slice thin, and bake on an ungreased cooky sheet in a moderate oven about 10 minutes. Before baking, decorate each cooky with a blanched almond. Other nuts or fruits may be used for decoration, but for the real French touch, use the almond.

These combine the excellent French flavor with the American ease of making, and are therefore most desirable.

Mme. Alcide Brasseur, Lancaster, Ohio.

PAIN D'EPICE

2 T lard	f.g. salt
1 egg	3 c chopped fruit
1 c B. sugar	(*This may include whatever*
½ c strong, black coffee	*you prefer of such things*
½ c dark corn syrup	*as orange and lemon peel,*
1 t cinnamon	*citron. raisins, nuts, candied*
1 t soda	*fruit, dates, currants, coco-*
3½ c flour	*nut, etc.*)

Cream the lard; add the egg and sugar, and blend well. Add the coffee and syrup, then the sifted-together, dry ingredients to which all the fruit and nuts have been added. Drop by teaspoonfuls on a greased cooky sheet, taking care that the raisins do not stick out from the tops of the cookies because they will burn. Bake in a slow oven about 15 minutes.

This makes a fruit-cake-like cooky, which is excellent with tea or coffee. By omitting one cup of the chopped fruit and baking it in loaf tins you may make a fruit loaf which is served by French people thus: Slice the loaf very thin and put the pieces together, sandwich fashion, with raspberry jam. The raspberry jam brings out the flavor of the *Pain d'Epice* in a special way and makes it much appreciated as a special sweet for the tea assortment.

Mrs. Fernand Pierre Brasseur, Lakewood, Ohio.

SUGAR CAKES

¼ c butter	¼ t lemon extract
¼ c C. sugar	1 c pastry flour
2 egg yolks	¼ t B.P.

Cream the butter and sugar; add the egg yolks, the flavoring, and beat. Add the flour and B.P., sifted together. Chill one hour. Roll very thin and cut. Sprinkle with G. sugar or finely chopped nuts. Bake in a moderate oven on a greased cooky sheet 8–10 minutes.

If placed in a covered tin, these will keep for a long time.

TWILLS

1 c sugar	½ c flour
3 eggs	f.g. salt
¾ c sliced almonds	

Mix the sugar, the beaten eggs and the salt. Add the flour and nuts. Drop at least two inches apart on a greased cooky sheet, and bake in a moderate oven 12–15 minutes. When they come from the oven, roll them at once around a wooden handle. They will keep this rolled shape if cooled at once. If you do not care to bother to shape the cooky, leave it in the flat form. It will taste just as good.

GERMANY

When one housewife says to another, "Are you making Christmas cookies this year?" she usually means, "Are you making German Christmas cookies this year?" German people in this country have passed their excellent recipes to the rest of us, and as the result of this we have gotten to appreciate such wonderful things as *Vanilla Sticks, Peppernuts, Lebkuchen, Anise Drops,* and *Springerle.*

In Germany great cooky bakings are held long before Christmas in order to have people around to help with the baking, to have plenty of time for the making of some of the more difficult recipes, and, above all, to give to many of the varieties time to ripen. People of German descent, in this country, look forward to the social time when they will get together to help with the beating, the shelling of nuts, and the chopping of fruit, but most of all, with that beating! It is not either unusual or burdensome for people who go in for this type of thing to make twenty different kinds of cookies.

Great variety is the most outstanding characteristic of the German cookies. Everyone's taste can be pleased with the chewy, honey, fruit cookies, the hard, dunking types, the highly flavored seed cookies, the delicate *Vanilla Sticks,* and the plain cookies which depend on interesting shape for their appeal. Everyone's pocketbook can also be pleased, since there are such expensive ones as *Hazelnut Drops* and such inexpensive ones as most of the seed cookies.

ALMOND CRESCENTS

1 c butter
1 c sugar
2 eggs
1 egg yolk

3 c flour
1 c finely ground, unblanched almonds
1 egg white for glaze

Cream the butter, add the sugar; and cream again. Add the beaten eggs and the egg yolk. Mix in the flour, and knead all into one large roll. Chill. Roll one-half inch thick and cut in crescents. Brush with the slightly beaten egg white. Sprinkle thickly with almonds, and bake on a greased cooky sheet in a slow oven 20 minutes.

ALMOND CRESCENTS
ALMOND PRETZELS

Crescents are attractive, rich, and easy to make. Do not serve them with a rich dessert.

ALMOND PRETZEL

½ c butter
1 c flour
¼ c sugar

2 beaten eggs
1 egg white
Ground almonds

Mix all into a piecrust-like dough. Form in pretzel shapes with the hands or a cooky press. Brush with slightly beaten egg white, and strew with finely ground almonds. Bake in a moderate oven on an ungreased cooky sheet 10 minutes.

These are attractive but fragile, and should be used soon after baking because of the amount of butter which will become stale.

ALMOND STICKS

½ c blanched, ground almonds	⅓ c sugar
	½ c flour
¼ t almond extract	1 egg
½ lemon rind, grated	

Mix in order, and pat thin on a square board. Cut in long sticks, and leave on the board overnight. Turn and leave four hours more. Bake on a greased cooky sheet in a moderate oven until slightly brown.

If a crisp cooky is desired, use them the day they are baked. If a soft one is preferred, let them stand in a cooky jar a day or two before using.

ANISE DROPS

3 eggs	1 c flour
1 c sugar	1½ T anise seed

Stir the sugar and eggs one-half hour (10 minutes in an electric beater). Add the flour and anise seed. Drop on a greased cooky sheet, and let them stand until a hard crust forms on top (about 8 hours). Bake in a moderate oven about 10 minutes. The tops will puff up to resemble icing.

These are popular with those who like the anise flavor. In a covered tin they will keep fresh a long time.

Elsie Schiefer, Bexley, Ohio.

ANISE SEED COOKIES

5 c flour	1 c shortening
2 c sugar	1 c sour milk
1 t salt	1 t soda
1 t B.P.	2 eggs
2 t anise seed	

Sift the dry ingredients and rub the shortening in as for pie dough. Add the milk, the seed, and the unbeaten eggs. Roll and cut. Bake on a greased cooky sheet in a moderate oven 10 minutes. They are crisp when first baked, but soften with age.

"They will keep a long time if you don't have three boys, and a girl, and your old man after them."

Mrs. John Kistemaker, Cleveland, Ohio.

ANISE SEED COOKIES

AUNT IDA'S TOUGHER ROLLS

AUNT IDA'S TOUGHER ROLLS

½ c Orleans molasses	⅔ c sugar
½ c butter	1 t ginger
1 c flour	

Heat the molasses to the boiling point. Add the butter and stir well. Add the sifted-together, dry ingredients, and drop on a greased cooky sheet, two inches apart, as they will run. Bake in a moderate oven 10 minutes. Carefully remove from the pan and roll at once into a tight roll, being careful that they remain in a warm place until they are rolled and are cooled immediately after the rolling takes place. If they begin to break during the rolling process, return them to the oven for a minute and start again. Place them on a brown paper to absorb the excess butter.

These are unique-looking and excellent, and as chewy as they are tasty.

Miss Ida M. Lintner, Lyndhurst Farm, Mechanicsburg, Ohio.

AUNT PAULINE'S CHRISTMAS BOXES

½ c butter	1½ c flour
¼ c sugar	1 square grated chocolate
f.g. salt	½ t vanilla
1 egg	

Cream the butter and add the sugar, chocolate, egg, vanilla, salt, and flour. Take three fourths of this mixture and form it into a long box, size twenty by two and one-half inches. Fill it with the filling and cover it with the rest of the first mixture made into a long, thin sheet which will just form the cover for the box. Pinch all the edges together so that the filling can't escape. Bake 45 minutes in a moderate oven. Slice thin and glaze.

FILLING

⅓ c sugar	2 c ground, unblanched
1 unbeaten egg white	almonds

Mix thoroughly.

GLAZE

1 c sugar	2 T lemon or other
	fruit juice

This recipe makes a large quantity of cookies, looking and tasting different, and are best served with a fancy assortment of tea cakes. They are rich and expensive to make, but worth it.

BRAZIL NUT STICKS

2 eggs	1 lb. Brazil nuts (shelled)
2 c B. sugar	½ t B.P.
1¾ c flour	1½ t vanilla

Beat the eggs until light; add the sugar, the vanilla, and beat again. Add the shelled and coarsely ground nuts to the sifted-together, dry ingredients. Blend both mixtures thoroughly. Let the dough stand in a cool place one or two hours. With the palms of the hands form rolls about three inches long. Bake on a greased cooky sheet in a moderate oven until delicately brown. When the sticks are cool, rub them in C. sugar.

These should be baked at least two weeks before Christmas. They keep well if packed in a covered tin. Their delicate flavor makes them fine with coffee or with frozen desserts or custards.

Mrs. A. W. Bradfield, Galion, Ohio.

CHOCOLATE MACAROONS

¾ c sugar
1 c unblanched almond
   strips
3 egg whites

2 t water
¼ lb. grated sweet
   chocolate
¼ t vanilla

Mix the sugar and water, and warm for half a minute over the fire. Add the almonds, and cool. Stir in the chocolate, the vanilla, and the unbeaten egg whites. Drop on a greased cooky sheet, and bake in a moderate oven 15 minutes. Cool before removing from the pan. Be careful in handling, as they crush easily.

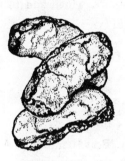

BRAZIL NUT STICKS

CINNAMON STARS

CHOCOLATE SNAPS

4 egg whites
1 square chocolate (grated)
½ t B.P.

1 c C. sugar
½ c flour
½ t vanilla

Beat the eggs and sugar 30 minutes (8–10 minutes in an electric beater). Add the other ingredients. Drop from a teaspoon on a greased cooky sheet at least two inches apart as they are thin and runny. Bake in a moderate oven 10 minutes.

These are crisp and thin. They keep well, and improve with age. Serve when a good, but not rich, cooky is wanted.

Elsie Schiefer, Bexley, Ohio.

CINNAMON STARS

2 egg whites
2/3 c sugar
1/2 t cinnamon

1/8 t cloves
2 c ground, unblanched
    almonds

Beat the eggs until very stiff. Add the sugar slowly and continue beating until the mixture is stiff enough to hold its shape. Stir in the spices and almonds, using enough almonds to make a soft dough. Mix 1/4 c flour and 1/4 c C. sugar for the rolling board. Roll the dough thin, and cut in star shape. Place on a greased cooky sheet and let dry for half an hour. Bake in a moderate oven 15 minutes. Watch closely, as they burn easily!

These are excellent, crisp, crunchy cookies, which add to the Christmas assortment because of their appropriate shape.

DOROTHEA LINDNER'S DUNKERS

1¾ c C. sugar
2 eggs
2½ c chopped nut meats
¼ c chopped citron
¼ c chopped orange peel

1½ c flour
¼ t soda
f.g. salt
½ t cinnamon
½ t cloves

Beat the eggs slightly, and add the sugar. Beat 10 minutes. Add the nuts and fruit to the sifted-together, dry ingredients. Add this to the first mixture. Blend well. Roll one-fourth inch thick. Cut in strips, and bake on a greased cooky sheet in a moderate oven 12 minutes. Glaze with fruit-juice glaze. (See page 174.)

These are best used as the name suggests. Store in jar.

EVERLASTING CAKES

2 c sugar
½ c honey
1 c milk or water
1 c chopped nuts

½ c chopped citron
½ t soda
½ t cinnamon
1 orange rind, grated

Boil the milk, sugar, and honey for 15 minutes, stirring often. Remove from the fire and add the nuts, fruit, and spices. Stir in as much flour as possible with a spoon. Let the mixture cool half an hour, then add the soda. Add enough additional flour to make a stiff dough. Let it stand overnight, or longer, in a cool place. The longer it stands, the less sticky it will be. Roll out one-third inch thick. Cut in fancy shapes, and bake on a greased cooky sheet in a moderate oven 10 minutes.

These will keep a year, if you let them!

FRUIT COOKIES

4 egg yolks	1 c chopped nuts
3 c sugar	2 c chopped dates
3 c dark corn syrup	1 box seedless raisins
1 t cinnamon	1 c warm milk
1 t cloves	2 t soda
1 t allspice	

Beat the egg yolks; add the sugar, corn syrup, spices, milk, and soda. Beat all together, then add 1 c of flour. Add the chopped fruit and nuts. Stir in enough additional flour to roll and cut in fancy shapes. Bake in a moderate oven on a greased cooky sheet 15–20 minutes. Frost with:

FROSTING

4 egg whites	1 t vanilla
1 lb. C. sugar (3⅔ c)	

These cookies are full of flavor, should never be used until at least a week old, and improve a great deal with age.

Mrs. Fred Pestel, New Albany, Ohio.

HAZELNUT BALLS

½ lb. shelled hazelnuts, ground (about 2 c)	1 lb. C. sugar (3⅔ c)
4 egg whites	½ lemon rind, grated

Beat the egg whites until they hold their shape. Add the sugar and continue to beat for 15 minutes (3–5 minutes in an electric beater). Save half this mixture for icing. Add the nuts and the lemon rind to the other half. Dip the hands in C. sugar and form small balls with the dough. Place them on a greased cooky sheet; make a dent in the center of each, and fill it with icing. Allow the balls to dry at least five minutes. Place on a greased cooky sheet, and bake in a slow oven until the icing is a delicate brown (about 15 minutes). Cool before removing from the pan.

These are much like the *Vanilla Sticks,* but with the distinctive flavor of hazelnuts. They keep well.

HAZELNUT BALLS

LEBKUCHEN

HAZELNUT COOKIES

2 eggs	½ t salt
1 c sugar	½ lemon rind, grated
1 c ground hazelnuts	2 c flour

Beat the yolks of the eggs until lemon colored, add the sugar gradually, and continue beating for five minutes. Add the ground nuts, salt, and lemon rind to the mixture. Add the flour and mix well. Fold in the stiffly beaten egg whites. Form small, round balls. Bake, one inch apart, on a greased cooky sheet in a moderate oven 10 minutes.

HAZELNUT MACAROONS

4 egg whites	1 c ground hazelnuts
2 egg yolks	⅛ t salt
½ c sugar	½ lemon rind, grated

Beat the yolks of the eggs until lemon colored. Add the sugar and continue beating for 10 minutes. Add the lemon rind and the nuts. Then add the salt to the egg whites, and beat until they are stiff. Fold them into the first mixture. Drop on a greased cooky sheet, and bake in a slow oven about 30 minutes. Remove from the pan while still hot.

This is a particularly delightful cooky for those who are especially fond of the hazelnut flavor.

LAPCUCHIA

3 c B. sugar	1 c raisins
2 c corn syrup	1 T ginger
(light or dark)	1 t cloves
3 egg yolks (save whites	1 t allspice
for icing)	2 t soda
1½ c chopped nuts	1 c warm, sweet milk
1 c finely chopped	Flour (about 7 c)
citron	

Mix the egg yolks and the sugar. Add the spices, nuts, raisins, and citron. Warm the syrup and add the soda to it. Stir in the first mixture. Add 2 c of flour alternately with the milk, then add more flour, as needed, to make a drop cooky dough. Spread one-half inch thick on a greased cooky sheet, and bake in a moderate oven 25 minutes or until the dough springs back when touched. Spread thinly with C. sugar glaze. (See page 174.) Return to the oven for one minute. Cut in two-inch squares.

These are not only good the day they are made, but they will keep for weeks. This recipe makes about four gallons of cookies, which is a lot for the modern family; but for the old-fashioned family, it was just enough to fill the cooky jar. A third of the amount would be right for this day and age.

Mrs. Paul Bruning, Gahanna, Ohio.

LEBKUCHEN No. 1

2 c sugar
4 eggs
⅔ c strained honey
1½ c unblanched almonds
5 c flour
½ t soda

1 t cinnamon
½ t allspice
1 t cloves
¾ c candied orange peel
¼ c candied lemon peel

Beat the sugar and the eggs until they are light and fluffy. Add the honey, then the almonds cut in long strips. Add the chopped peel to the sifted-together, dry ingredients. Combine the two mixtures. Chill well. Spread on a greased cooky sheet as thick as desired, and bake in a moderate oven about 30 minutes. Place the sheet on a cooky rack or a sheet of waxed paper, and cover with lemon glaze. (See page 174.) When cool, cut in squares or strips. Store with an orange in cooky jar.

These are delicious and improve with age.

LEBKUCHEN No. 2

2 c honey
½ c sugar
1 T cinnamon
1 T soda
1 wine glass of
   whisky (¼ c)
Juice of 1 lemon
1 c finely chopped citron

1 c blanched almond strips,
   roasted with
1 T sugar
3 egg yolks
8 c flour
3 egg whites (for C. sugar
   frosting, p. 172)

Bring the honey to a boil; add the sugar and cool. Add the cinnamon, the soda stirred in the whisky, the lemon juice, and the citron. Add the egg yolks and the flour to make the dough. Lay the roasted almonds on a board, and cover with the dough. Let stand overnight. Next morning roll out one-fourth inch thick, cut in strips, and bake (almond side down) on a greased cooky sheet in a moderate oven 12–15 minutes. Frost with icing while warm. Store with an orange in cooky jar.

Mrs. Esther Althauser Boehm, Westerville, Ohio.

LEPP COOKIES

5 eggs
2 c sugar
½ c finely chopped
   citron
½ c finely chopped
   orange peel

½ c chopped nuts
   (or coconut)
½ t cinnamon
½ t cloves
1 t cream of tartar
3 c flour

Beat the eggs; add the sugar slowly, and beat again. Add the sifted-together, dry ingredients and the fruit and nuts. Spread one-fourth inch thick on a greased cooky sheet, and bake in a moderate oven 15–20 minutes. Remove and cool slightly. Spread with a thin coating of icing made of lemon juice and C. sugar. When cold, cut in two-inch squares.

These are crisp when baked, but soften after they stand. They should be kept a week, at least, before serving; and they will keep much longer. The flavor, though similar to Lebkuchen, is different. They are fine with hot or cold beverages.

Martha Lantz, New Albany, Ohio.

NÜRNBERGERS

NÜRNBERGER

1 c honey
¾ c B. sugar
1 egg
1 T lemon juice
1 t grated lemon rind
1 t grated orange rind
2½ c flour
½ t soda

1½ t cinnamon
½ t allspice
½ t cloves
½ c chopped citron
½ c chopped nuts
Whole blanched almonds and
   pieces of citron for
   decorating

Bring the honey to a boil. Remove from the fire and add the sugar. Cool thoroughly. Add the beaten egg, lemon, and orange rind. Sift the dry ingredients. Add the chopped fruit and nuts; then add all to the honey mixture. Form in two long rolls three inches in diameter. Let stand in a cool place all night. In the morning slice into thin rounds and decorate each with the almonds and citron to imitate the petals of a daisy. These nuts and citron must be stuck on to the cookie with a drop of honey, otherwise they will fall off after baking. Bake on a greased cooky sheet in a

PEPPERNUTS

moderate oven 15 minutes. Do not use them until they have ripened in a cooky jar at least a week. They are just as good at the end of a month.

These are most attractive in the Christmas collection in spite of their large size. People who don't care for the distinctive flavor of anise and caraway will welcome them.

PEPPERNUTS

4 eggs	½ t allspice
2 c G. sugar	¼ t cloves
¼ lb. finely chopped citron (½ c)	½ t pepper
2 t cinnamon	4 c flour

Mix the eggs and sugar and beat one hour (15 minutes in an electric mixer). Add the rest of the ingredients to the mixture. More flour may be added if needed for rolling. Roll thin; cut in small rounds. Place them on a board. Let them stand all night. Next morning turn them, putting a drop of water on the top of each cooky. Bake on a greased cooky sheet in a slow oven 15 minutes. The tops will puff.

They are very hard when baked, but should be kept at least a week before they are used. They will be softer and much esteemed by those who have cultivated their flavor for coffee dunking, morning or afternoon.

Mrs. Leo Schott, New Albany, Ohio.

POTTSDAM CAKES

1 c sugar	2 eggs
½ c butter	⅔ c milk
2½ c flour	½ t flavoring
2 t B.P.	

Mix the sugar, butter, and flavoring. Add the beaten eggs and the milk. Add the sifted-together, dry ingredients. Drop on a greased cooky sheet, and bake in a moderate oven 10–12 minutes. They may be decorated. If a small gem pan is used, decrease the flour ½ cup.

These are inexpensive and good, but must be used soon after baking.

RICH ALMOND COOKIES

⅔ c butter	3 c flour
½ c sugar	½ t vanilla
½ c unblanched, ground almonds	

Cream the butter and sugar. Add the almonds and vanilla. Mix in the flour, and knead. Form into little balls, and flatten down on a cooky sheet. Bake in a moderate oven 10 minutes. While still warm, sprinkle with G. sugar.

These are very rich, but decidedly good.

"S" COOKIES

4 c flour	½ lemon rind, grated
1 c butter	6 egg yolks
½ c sugar	

Work the ingredients together as for piecrust. Form small S-shaped cookies with the hands or a cooky press which has a pastry tube attachment. Any other shape may be used but the "S" is traditional. Sprinkle with G. sugar (red or green is nice at Christmas), and bake on an ungreased cooky sheet in a hot oven 10 minutes. These should be used soon after baking as the great quantity of butter spoils with age.

They are popular with those who like a very rich, buttery-flavored cooky. It is clever, when packing a Christmas box, to form the initials of the person who is to receive the box. Or, if the cookies are for the family, an initial for each member is interesting and flattering.

Elsie Schiefer, Bexley, Ohio.

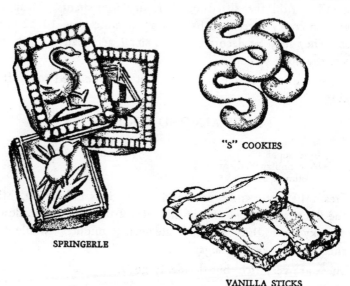

"S" COOKIES

SPRINGERLE

VANILLA STICKS

SPRINGERLE

4 eggs	½ t anise oil (more, if
2 c G. sugar	stronger flavor is desired)
5–6 c flour	

Beat the eggs until lemon colored, then add the sugar and continue beating for one hour (15 minutes in an electric mixer). Add the anise oil and enough flour to make a dough which will roll. Roll about one-half inch thick and press the sheet with a

Springerle board or pin (any shape will do if these are not available). Let these cookies dry overnight on the greased cooky sheet. Next morning bake them in a moderate oven. The tops will puff to resemble icing but will retain the shape of the design. They are hard at first, but soften a bit with age.

Anise seed may be substituted for the oil, but this makes the design of the cooky less accurate. Coffee drinkers and dunkers are fond of these. Store with an orange in jar.

Mrs. Leo Schott, New Albany, Ohio.

VANILLA STICKS

1 lb. shelled almonds (4 c)	2 lbs. C. sugar (7⅓ c)
8 egg whites	1 vanilla bean

Beat the eggs until they are stiff enough to hold their shape. Add the sugar and beat 15 minutes (3–5 minutes in an electric beater). Set aside one half of the mixture for the icing. Add the unblanched, ground almonds, along with the finely ground vanilla bean, to the rest of the mixture. Roll out thin on a floured board. Cut in thin strips, and spread with the icing. Let them dry five minutes, then place close together (they do not run) on a greased cooky sheet. Bake in a slow oven 15 minutes or until the icing is delicately brown. Cool before removing from pan.

Of the fancy German Christmas cookies, these are perhaps the most liked. They are the most popular on the plate or in the box of assorted varieties, and are delicious alone or with any beverage or dessert. They keep well if packed in tin.

Elsie Schiefer, Bexley, Ohio.

HEBREW

HONEY CORN CAKES
MANDEL SLICES

To the palate that is not used to these flavors and textures, the Hebrew cookies seem the most unusual of all. It takes some cultivation to think of poppy seeds, pepper, and corn meal as ingredients for cookies, but the taste can be educated and will find these things all worth while.

Outstanding is the great use of honey, which we might expect, since it is a sweet which is older than the Bible itself, and a good one, too, as it makes the cookies keep a long time.

We are used to seeds in the German and English cookies, but not in such quantities as they appear here.

Unusual is the method employed in the making of some of the cookies—notably the *Tayglech* and the *Honey Corn Cakes.* But they are fairly simple to make, and the result justifies the labor for many people.

100

The texture of all of these is very hard and compact in comparison to the fluffiness of most of the American varieties. That is the usual criticism of a person who tastes them the first time. But again, it is possible to cultivate a taste.

ALMOND COOKIES

1 c ground, unblanched almonds	¼ c butter
	¼ c sugar

Mix all and form into a long roll. Chill. Cut in thin rounds, and bake in a moderate oven 12–16 minutes. Watch to prevent burning.

These are fine after they are baked, and just as good a week later, if you can restrain yourself from eating that long.

ANISE SPONGE DROPS

5 eggs	1 t B.P.
1 c sugar	½ t vanilla
1 t water	2 T anise seeds
2 c flour	

Mix the egg yolks, sugar, water, and vanilla; then beat well. Add the sifted-together, dry ingredients and the seeds. Fold in the stiffly beaten egg whites. Drop on a greased cooky sheet, and bake in a moderate oven 20–25 minutes.

Donna Gitlin, Columbus, Ohio.

CHOCOLATE NUT COOKIES

3 egg whites	1 c ground walnuts
¾ c C. sugar	¼ c flour
1 c grated sweet chocolate	

Mix all but the egg whites; then add them unbeaten, and mix well. Drop in small mounds on a greased cooky sheet, and bake in a slow oven 10–12 minutes.

FOAM COOKIES

2 egg whites
1 c C. sugar

2 c finely chopped almonds

Beat the egg whites until they are stiff and dry. Add the sugar gradually, then the nuts. Drop two inches apart, on a greased cooky sheet, and bake in a moderately slow oven 12 minutes. Remove from the pan when cold.

These are like large, flat macaroons.

HONEY COOKIES

1/4 c honey
1/4 c sifted C. sugar
1/2 c unblanched, chopped
    almonds
1/2 c flour

1 T chopped citron
1 lemon rind, grated
1/8 t nutmeg
1/8 t cloves
1/2 wine-glass brandy (2 T)

Warm the honey and the sugar. Work in the rest of the ingredients. Chill one week. Roll one-half inch thick, cut, and bake on a greased cooky sheet in a moderate oven 15 minutes.

These are crisp when baked, but soften and are better as they stand.

HONEY CORN CAKES

1/2 c honey
1/2 c corn meal
1/8 t each, allspice,
    cloves, pepper

2 T brandy
1/4 c flour
1/2 c chopped nuts

Heat the honey and add the rest of the ingredients. Knead, using white flour. Drop on a greased cooky sheet and place a drop of brandy on top of each cooky. Bake in a moderate oven 15 minutes. Watch to prevent burning. While still warm, dust with C. sugar.

These are very unusual, and will not be liked by those who do not care for unusual things.

HONEY CRACKERS

2 c flour
f.g. salt
2 eggs
½ t allspice

⅔ t soda
1 t lemon juice
½ lemon rind, grated
2 T honey

Mix the dry ingredients; add the lemon rind, juice, honey, and the unbeaten eggs. Beat well. Roll thin and cut. Bake on a greased cooky sheet in a moderate oven 15 minutes.

These are good, but not sweet. If a sweeter cooky is desired, they should be iced with C. sugar and lemon juice icing. Do not keep them long as they dry out.

MANDEL SLICES

3 eggs
½ c sugar
1½ t B.P.

1½ c flour
½ c finely chopped almonds
2 T melted butter

Beat well the eggs and sugar. Add the dry ingredients, the nuts, and the melted butter. Pour into a greased, square cake pan, and bake in a moderate oven 30–35 minutes. Cool, and cut in slices. Sprinkle with C. sugar.

Donna Gitlin, Columbus, Ohio.

NUTMEG DROPS

2 c flour
½ c sugar
½ t B.P.
1 lemon rind, grated

2 eggs
1 t nutmeg
1 T chopped citron
1 t cinnamon

Work into a dough. Form into small balls. Bake on a greased cooky sheet, in a moderate oven, 12–15 minutes. While still warm, roll in C. sugar.

These are much like *Peppernuts* in taste and appearance, with the nutmeg taking the place of the pepper. Store in cooky jar.

PARVE COOKIES

2 c flour
½ t B.P.
2 eggs
½ c poppy seeds

2 T shortening
1 c sugar
f.g. salt

Mix the dry ingredients and the seeds. Add the beaten eggs and the softened shortening. Flatten onto a square cake pan. Bake in a moderate oven until brown (about 10 minutes). Cut in squares.

Donna Gitlin, Columbus, Ohio.

PRUNE COOKIES

1½ c flour
½ t salt
1½ t B.P.

½ c sweet cream
1 egg
½ c melted butter

FILLING

½ lb. cooked prunes,
stoned and cut up (1 c)

2 T sugar
½ t cinnamon

Mix the dry ingredients. Add the liquids and mix into a dough for rolling. Roll thin and cut out rounds. Place a spoonful of filling on the center of each cooky. Fold the edges together to form a long, filled cooky, with a small opening in the middle. Bake on a greased cooky sheet in a moderate oven 20–25 minutes.

Use soon after baking as they do not keep well.

Donna Gitlin, Columbus, Ohio.

RAISIN DROPS

2 eggs
2 c sugar
2½ T melted butter
1 t vanilla

1 c milk
3 c flour
2 t B.P.
½ c seedless raisins

Beat the eggs, sugar, and butter for 10 minutes. Add the rest in the order given and drop on a greased cooky sheet. Bake in a moderate oven about 10 minutes.

Donna Gitlin, Columbus, Ohio.

TAYGLECH

DOUGH

1 egg   ¼ t B.P.
⅔ c flour

HONEY MIXTURE

¼ c honey   ¼ c chopped walnuts
¼ c sugar   Finely chopped walnuts
¼ t ginger   for rolling

Mix the egg, flour, and B.P. into a dough. Knead well. Form
into a long roll one inch thick. Slice off thin pieces and drop
into the honey mixture which has boiled one minute. Continue
boiling until each piece is brown and caramel-looking. Remove
from the fire. Drop all the pieces in cold water, and then roll
them in the finely chopped walnuts. Put on a board to dry.

This sounds impossible, but it is really not difficult. They
keep a long time, and are delicious if you like that sort of
different thing.   *Donna Gitlin*, Columbus, Ohio.

TRICORNS

DOUGH

½ c melted butter   ½ t salt
½ c sugar   2½ c flour
1 egg   3 t B.P.
¼ c milk

Mix all the ingredients and knead well. Roll thin. Cut in large
rounds. Put a spoonful of filling in the center of each round and
fold the edges up so as to form a tricorn. Pinch them together.
Bake on a greased cooky sheet in a moderate oven about 20
minutes.

FILLING

1 egg   ½ c poppy seeds
¾ c sugar

Mix well.

These are neither very sweet nor rich, but they are good with
a beverage, particularly coffee.

HOLLAND

JORDAN ALMOND COOKIES
DUTCH ALMOND SLICES

Dutch cookies are generally quite rich, but very tasty, due to the use of nuts (especially almonds), wine, and brandy, which give the cookies special flavor. They are easy to make. Most of them may be adapted to our modern icebox methods.

Since the Dutch probably gave us the word "cookies," we expect theirs to be worth while. We are not disappointed.

ALMOND COOKIES

½ c butter	½ c blanched almond
½ c lard	slices
½ c G. sugar	¼ t cinnamon
½ c B. sugar	¼ t nutmeg
2 eggs	½ t soda
	3 c flour

Cream the butter, lard, and sugars. Add the eggs, and mix well. Add the sifted-together, dry ingredients and the nuts. Mold into a long roll and let stand in the icebox or other cool place overnight. Slice thin, and bake on a cooky sheet in a hot oven, about 10 minutes or until brown.

These are rich, have a wonderful flavor, and come from the recipe brought from Holland by the ancestors of Mrs. Florence Gillcrist, of Rock Island, Illinois.

HONEY COOKIES

1½ c flour	¼ t cloves
⅛ c sugar	¼ c brandy, wine, or
¼ c honey	other fruit juice
1 t B.P.	¼ c grated citron
¼ t cinnamon	

Boil the honey and sugar. Stir in the spices and citron; remove from the fire. Cool. Add the brandy and dry ingredients. Roll thin; cut into shapes, and bake on a greased cooky sheet in a moderate oven 10–12 minutes.

They are hard at first but, like all honey cookies, improve with age.

JORDAN ALMOND COOKIES

½ c candy Jordan	¼ c sugar
almonds, ground fine	3 eggs
1 c ground, unblanched	2 ground cracknel
almonds	biscuits

Beat the sugar and the egg yolks one minute. Fold in the beaten egg whites. Stir in the ground biscuits and the nuts. Drop on a greased cooky sheet, and bake in a moderate oven 10 minutes.

These are like macaroons, but have an odd flavor from the Jordan almonds and the cracknel biscuits.

"KOCKIES"

2 c flour	½ c ground nuts
¾ c B. sugar	1 egg
¼ c butter	½ t cloves
1 T other shortening	1 T wine
1 t cinnamon	½ t soda

Rub the butter and fat into the flour. Add the sugar, nuts and spices; then mix. Add the soda dissolved in 2 T water, the egg, and the wine. Drop on a greased cooky sheet, and bake in a moderate oven 10–15 minutes.

These are rich and good, with a special flavor from the wine.

MOLASSES COOKY ROLLS

¼ c dark corn syrup	½ t B.P.
¼ c Orleans molasses	¼ t soda
⅔ c sugar	⅛ t salt
¼ c butter	½ t lemon juice
¼ c lard	½ lemon rind, grated
1¼ c flour	

Heat the corn syrup, molasses, and sugar. Add the lemon juice and rind, the butter and lard, and the salt. Remove from the fire, and add the sifted-together, dry ingredients. Stir well. Set the pan in a bowl of hot water. Drop by teaspoonfuls at least two inches apart (they are very thin and will run). Bake on a greased cooky sheet in a moderate oven 10 minutes or until crisp. Remove from the oven, and form into rolls while they are still warm. If they break in the rolling process, return them to the oven and start again as soon as they are warmed.

They are much like the German, English, and American rolled cookies.

SOUTH AFRICAN CLARET COOKIES

¾ c B. sugar	½ t soda in 1 t warm water
⅓ c shortening (½ butter and ½ lard)	¼ t cinnamon
	⅛ t cloves
2 c flour	½ c chopped, unblanched almonds
2 egg yolks	
2 T claret	

Mix the sugar and shortening; add the eggs, claret, spice, and soda. Mix. Add the nuts and flour. Drop on a greased cooky sheet, and bake in a moderate oven 12–15 minutes. Fruit juice may be used for claret, but the flavor will be slightly changed.

SPRITZ

⅜ c sugar
¼ c butter
½ t vanilla

1 egg
1 c flour
1 t B.P.

Cream the butter. Add the sugar and the unbeaten egg, then beat again. Add the vanilla and the sifted-together, dry ingredients. Mold with a cooky press or drop in balls, and bake on a greased cooky sheet in a moderate oven 10 minutes.

VAN NESS SWEETS

½ c butter
1 c B. sugar (dark)
1 cake compressed yeast
dissolved in
1 t warm water

3 c flour
2 t cinnamon
1 t allspice
1 t salt
4 eggs

Mix all in the order given, and knead. Let rise in a warm place half an hour. Roll three-fourths inch thick; cut in rounds, and bake in a slow oven until brown. Ice with lemon-C.sugar icing. Decorate with candied peel or nuts.

These will keep for days and are good with beverages, especially wines.

WINE WAFERS

1 c flour
½ c sugar
¼ c butter
4 eggs

2 t cinnamon
¼ c wine (any kind, or fruit
juice may be used)

Cream the butter and sugar. Beat in the eggs one at a time, adding a tablespoonful of flour after each egg. Stir in the cinnamon, the wine, and the rest of the flour. Drop by small teaspoonfuls on a greased cooky sheet two inches apart, as they spread, and bake in a hot oven 5–10 minutes. Dredge with cinnamon and C. sugar. Remove at once from pan.

These may be baked on a waffle iron and cut in squares. They are very crisp and not at all rich, so they may be served with a very rich dessert.

HUNGARY

POPPY SEED STRIPS
LADY FINGERS

Hungarians are good cooks. We have this assurance on the word of a Hungarian woman herself. Be that as it may, we have reasons to agree with her. Anything which uses as much jam, as many nuts (and remember that all real Hungarian cookies use the almonds unblanched), as much rich chocolate, and as many eggs as these cookies, ought to be most delicious.

ALMOND HORNS

1 c butter	1 c unblanched, ground
1 c sugar	almonds
2 c flour	1 t vanilla
	f.g. salt

Mix the butter, sugar, flour, and salt. Add the nuts and vanilla. With the hands form tiny horns, flattening them slightly on a greased cooky sheet by pressing them gently with the tines of a fork. Bake in a moderate oven 10 minutes, and roll, while they are still warm, in C. sugar.

These may be made as icebox cookies, but the first method is more typically Hungarian.

Mrs. Rose Tulea, Cleveland, Ohio.

ALMOND SQUARES

1 c flour
½ c sugar
1 egg
⅛ t salt

Chopped, unblanched
almonds
1 egg yolk (for glaze)

Mix the dry ingredients; stir in the egg. Put half the dough on a greased, square cake pan. Sprinkle with almonds. Press the other half on top, and brush with the egg yolk diluted with 1 T water. Bake in a moderate oven 10–15 minutes, and mark in squares while still warm.

ALMOND WAFERS

½ c butter
½ c sugar
1 egg
½ c finely ground,
    unblanched almonds

½ lemon rind, grated
½ t each, cinnamon, cloves,
    and nutmeg
2 c flour
½ t almond extract

Cream the butter and sugar, then add the egg beaten until frothy. Stir in the rest of the ingredients. Form in long rolls. Chill overnight. Slice thin, and bake on a greased cooky sheet in a moderate oven 5–8 minutes. These must be only faintly brown.

Mrs. Rose Tulea, Cleveland, Ohio.

BUTTER-NUT WREATHS

½ c sugar
½ c butter
1 c flour

2 egg yolks
½ t vanilla
1 egg yolk ⎰mixed, for
1 T water ⎱brushing

Cream the butter and sugar. Add the vanilla and the unbeaten egg yolks. Beat well. Add the flour. Roll thin and cut as for doughnuts. Brush with the egg yolk and water. Sprinkle with any kind of nuts, and bake until golden brown in a slow oven.
These are better if used soon after they are made.

CHOCOLATE COOKIES

½ c shortening	¼ c milk
1½ c sugar	2 t B.P.
2½ c flour	2 squares chocolate
1 egg	¼ t salt

Cream the shortening and sugar; add the milk and egg mixed. Add the melted chocolate, then the dry ingredients. Form into long rolls; chill overnight; slice thin and decorate the top of each cooky with an unblanched almond. Bake in a moderate oven 10–12 minutes.

These can be made in icebox molds, but the shape has nothing to do with the delicious flavor. They keep well.

Mrs. Rose Tulea, Cleveland, Ohio.

CHOCOLATE KISSES

2 egg whites	¼ t vanilla
1 square of chocolate	f.g. salt
½ c sugar	

Add the salt to the egg whites and beat until they are firm. Slowly add the sugar a spoonful at a time, beating after each addition. Add the vanilla and the melted chocolate. Drop on a greased cooky sheet, and bake in a slow oven about 45 minutes or until the kisses are firm and dry. Heat the pan a bit if they will not come off easily. Sprinkle with G. sugar.

COFFEE DROPS

6 egg yolks	¼ c finely pulverized coffee
1⅓ c C. sugar	6 egg whites
2½ c ground, unblanched almonds	1 t vanilla

Beat the egg yolks until thick and lemon colored. Add the sugar, almonds, coffee, and vanilla. Last, fold in the stiffly beaten egg whites. Drop on a greased tin, and bake in a slow oven 30 minutes.

Mrs. Rose Tulea, Cleveland, Ohio.

CREAMY PUFF KISSES

5 egg whites	½ t vanilla
2½ c sugar	f.g. salt

Beat the egg whites and salt until very stiff. Add the sugar gradually, continuing the beating. Add the vanilla. Fill small, greased muffin pans two thirds full, and bake in a slow oven 30 minutes.

FARINA DROPS

6 egg yolks	1 c farina or other
1 c sugar	similar cereal
2 c finely ground,	1 t B.P.
unblanched almonds	6 egg whites

Beat the egg yolks and sugar until they are lemon colored. Add almonds, then the farina mixed with the B.P. Fold in the stiffly beaten egg whites. Drop on a greased and floured cooky sheet, and bake in a slow oven 25–30 minutes.

Mrs. Rose Tulea, Cleveland, Ohio.

HUNGARIAN SURPRISES

4 eggs	1 c flour
f.g. salt	1 lemon rind, grated
¾ c sugar	

Beat the egg yolk and the sugar. Add the lemon rind. Beat the whites of eggs and salt until stiff and dry, and fold in the first mixture. Add the flour slowly. Bake in a greased and floured muffin tin in a slow oven until the cakes are slightly brown, and remove very cautiously from the pan. Make a little hole in the center of each cake and fill it with jam or whipped cream.. Stop up the hole with a nut, and cover the whole thing with chocolate glaze.

These are attractive and unusual, but should be used as soon as they are made as they do not keep well.

LADY FINGERS

5 eggs	¼ t vanilla
½ c sugar	⅛ t salt
1 c pastry flour	

Separate the eggs. Add the salt to the whites and beat them to a foam. Add the vanilla; slowly add the sugar, beating after each addition. Then add the beaten egg yolks. Sift the flour in slowly. Form lady fingers on a greased and floured cooky sheet. Sprinkle with sugar or ground nuts, and bake in a hot oven 5–7 minutes. Remove and cool. Serve soon after baking.

NUT COOKIES

¾ c ground, unblanched almonds	6 eggs
¾ c fine, dry bread crumbs	1 c sugar

Beat the egg yolks and sugar 20 minutes (3–5 minutes in an electric mixer). Add half the almonds and all the bread crumbs. Fold in the stiffly beaten egg whites. Drop on a greased cooky sheet, and sprinkle each cooky with the rest of the nuts. Bake in a moderate oven 10–15 minutes.

Mrs. Rose Tulea, Cleveland, Ohio.

POPPY SEED STRIPS

3 egg yolks	1 T ground raisins
⅜ c sugar	½ T ground citron
½ c ground poppy seeds	½ t vanilla
⅛ c ground, unblanched almonds	3 egg whites
	½ lemon rind, grated

Beat the egg yolks and sugar until light. Add the rest of the ingredients and fold in the stiffly beaten egg whites. Pour an inch thick on a greased cooky sheet, sprinkle thickly with fine bread crumbs. Bake in a slow oven until set and brown. Cool. Cut in strips, and serve at once.

Mrs. Rose Tulea, Cleveland, Ohio.

SUGAR COOKIES

¼ c lard	3 c flour
1 c butter	f.g. salt
1 c sugar	1 lemon rind, grated
2 eggs	

Mix all as for piecrust, reserving 1 egg white for brushing. "When all are mixt, it will look like a rich dough, but never fear, get your dough board out, flour it lightly and place the dough on the board." Pinch off pieces of dough; toss them in the flour, and place them on a greased cooky sheet. Flatten with a fork, place a maraschino cherry in the middle of each, glaze with egg white, and bake in a hot oven 10 minutes.

Mrs. Rose Tulea, Cleveland, Ohio.

YELLOW MOONS

1 c sugar	f.g. salt
1 c butter	1¾ c flour
1 c milk	½ t almond extract
6 eggs	

Cream the butter, sugar, and egg yolks. Add the dry ingredients alternately with the milk and flavoring. Fold in the stiffly beaten egg whites, and pour onto a greased cooky sheet one-half inch thick. Sprinkle thickly with unblanched, ground almonds. Bake in a moderate oven 15 minutes. Cool and cut in moon shapes.

These may be frosted or glazed if a fancier cooky is wanted. They should be used soon after baking.

Mrs. Rose Tulea, Cleveland, Ohio.

VARGA KISSES

2 egg whites	½ c finely cut almonds
½ c sugar	or walnuts
f.g. salt	½ c finely cut dates

Beat the egg whites, slowly adding the sugar and salt gradually for 35–40 minutes, (about 10 minutes in an electric mixer). The mass should be smooth and thick. Add the dates and nuts. Drop by teaspoonfuls on a greased and floured cooky sheet and bake in a slow oven until light yellow, but not brown (about 15–20 minutes). Cool slightly and remove from the pan, being careful not to crush.

These are simple to make, attractive and delicious.

Mrs. Irene Varga Gibbons, Cleveland, Ohio.

IRELAND

BUTTER SHAMROCKS

It is possible that the various parts of the British Isles may resent knowing that there are very definite points of resemblance in the cookies of those various parts. But after much testing and tasting, there is no other conclusion to be drawn.

Here is the shortbread, the spice, the fruit, and the nuts, but all with a slight difference. Here, also, is the green shamrock, which is like nothing else in the world except Ireland. You'll like them all. You can't help it when they're so good.

BUTTER SHAMROCKS

½ c butter	2 t B.P.
1 c sugar	1 t flavoring
2 well-beaten eggs	Flour, enough to roll
1 T milk	(about 1½ c)
½ t salt	

Cream the butter; add the sugar, eggs, milk and one cup of the flour sifted with the B.P. and salt. Add enough additional flour to make the dough easy to roll. Add the flavoring. Chill. Roll thin. Cut with shamrock cutter. Brush with egg white, and sprinkle with green sugar. The latter may be bought, or it can be made by mixing green coloring with G. sugar and allowing it to dry. Bake on a greased cooky sheet in a moderate oven 10 minutes.

These are especially fine and appropriate at St. Patrick's Day luncheons.

CRISP SPICE COOKIES

½ c shortening	2⅔ c flour
1 c B. sugar	½ t soda
1 unbeaten egg	2 t B.P.
½ c dark corn syrup	1½ t cinnamon
½ c sour milk	f.g. salt
½ c chopped raisins	1½ t ginger
⅓ c chopped citron	

Cream the shortening and sugar. Add the egg, corn syrup, and milk. Mix well and add the sifted-together, dry ingredients and the fruits. Drop on a greased cooky sheet, and bake in a moderate oven 12 minutes.

These are fine. Coconut may be substituted for the citron and the result is good—better for those who don't care for the citron flavor.

DUNDEE STRIPS

½ c butter	¼ c chopped raisins
½ c sugar	1 slice finely cut, candied
1½ c flour	pineapple
2 eggs	⅛ c finely cut, candied
1 t B.P.	cherries (maraschino, if
¼ c candied peel	that flavor is preferred)
¼ c chopped nuts	

Cream the butter and sugar. Add the beaten eggs. Sift half the flour with the B.P. and add to the mixture. Dredge the fruit with the rest of the flour, and add. Pat on a greased pan until one inch thick. Bake in a slow oven 25–30 minutes. Cool and glaze with lemon glaze. Cut in finger-like strips.

These are delicious fruit cookies—fine for tea.

Mrs. Mary Lintner Lewis, Rio Grande, Ohio.

GINGER SHORTBREAD

2 c flour	½ c butter
½ c B. sugar	1½ t ginger
1½ t B.P.	2 t water

Cream the butter and sugar. Add the water and the sifted-together, dry ingredients. This will be a creamy, but stiff, mixture. Work with the hands to get it in shape so that it may be forced onto a square, greased cake pan about one-half inch thick. Press pieces of preserved ginger into the top of the short bread. Bake in a slow oven 20 minutes. Cut in squares while still warm, but do not remove from the pan until cool.

GREAT GRANDMOTHER'S PLUM COOKIES

½ c butter	⅛ c candied cherries
½ c sugar	1 t B.P.
1 egg	⅔ c currants
1 T water	⅓ c candied peel
2 c flour	

Cream the butter and sugar. Add the unbeaten egg, then the water. Mix the fruit and dredge it with half the flour. Mix the remainder of the flour with the B.P. and add to the mixture. Then add the fruit. Drop on a greased cooky sheet, and bake in a slow oven 25 minutes.

IRISH SHORTBREAD

1 c butter	4 c flour
1 c sugar	2 T finely chopped almonds
½ c whole, blanched almonds	

Cream the butter and sugar. Work in the flour and the chopped almonds. Press in a thin layer on a cooky sheet. Cover with the whole almonds, and bake in a slow oven 10 minutes. Remove from the oven, and cut in strips. Return to the oven and continue baking until all is evenly browned.

This makes a large quantity. For the average family, half the recipe would be enough.

PEANUT BUTTER KISSES

½ c peanut butter
2 T chopped peanuts
1 c chopped dates

¾ c C. sugar
2 unbeaten egg whites

Stir all the ingredients until they are well blended. Drop on a greased cooky sheet, and decorate the top of each cooky with a peanut. Bake in a moderate oven 15 minutes. Watch to prevent burning. Raisins or currants may be substituted for the dates.

These are good and chewy, and popular with those who like peanuts.

SNAPS

1 c butter
2 c sugar
1 egg
1 grated lemon or orange
     rind

2 t nutmeg
1 c water
¼ c brandy or wine
5 c flour

Cream the butter and sugar well. Add the rest in the order given. Mix well and chill one-half hour. Roll very thin. Cut in shapes and bake on a greased cooky sheet in a moderately hot oven about 10 minutes.

These are delightfully crisp and well flavored. For St. Patrick's Day, sprinkle them with green sugar before baking.

ITALY

SICILIAN SLICES
TEA BALLS
MANTUAN WAFERS

The poorer classes in Italy, as in most other countries, do not have the money to spend on such luxuries as cookies. They do well to have the mainstays of life. Once in a while, for a feast day, perhaps, they celebrate with little cakes like our cookies.

But the wealthy have their cakes and cookies to go along with a custard or ice-cream dessert. Some places they serve afternoon tea at which the cooky has its place. One notices a similarity in the cookies of most of the nations where such luxuries are meant primarily for the upper classes.

It is known that French chefs have influenced those of Russia, Italy, and even the Scotch and English. There is a tendency to put the emphasis on decoration rather than into the body of the cooky—to give it that "dressed up" holiday look.

120

But they're all good. Made of dried fruits, nuts, wine, and all sorts of candied peels and fruits, what could help but make them tasty?

CREAM PUFFS

½ c butter	1 c flour
1 c boiling water	f.g. salt
4 eggs	

Put the butter, salt, and water in a pan and heat to the boiling point. Add the flour, and stir over the fire until the mixture all forms into a ball. Cool a little, then add the unbeaten eggs one at a time, mixing each one in thoroughly before the other one is added. Place in very small mounds on a greased cooky sheet, and brush with egg yolk diluted with a little milk. Bake in a moderate oven 30–35 minutes. Be sure they are well dried out inside before they are removed from the oven or they will sink. Cool. Cut a slit in the side, and fill with flavored whipped cream or *Cream Filling*.

CREAM FILLING

¾ c sugar	2 eggs
⅓ c flour	2 c scalded milk
½ t salt	1 t vanilla

Mix the dry ingredients and add the scalded milk gradually. Cook over a low flame until the mixture thickens, stirring constantly. Add the mixture to the beaten eggs and stir. Cool and add the flavoring.

Sprinkle the tiny puffs with C. sugar, and you have a most attractive dessert which should be used soon after baking.

Mrs. Josephine DiTirro Baker, Portsmouth, Ohio.

CREMONA HONEY CAKES

½ c honey	½ lemon rind, grated
½ c chopped, blanched almonds	⅔ c flour

Boil the honey and almonds slowly 5 minutes, stirring all the while. Add the flour and lemon rind, and roll at once into a thin dough. Cut in rounds, and bake on a greased cooky sheet in a moderate oven 5–8 minutes.

These are hard after baking, but will soften in a week into a good, chewy cooky which keeps well.

FIG HONEY COOKIES

FILLED COOKIES

FIG HONEY COOKIES

½ c shortening	1 t B.P.
¾ c sugar	1 t lemon extract
2 eggs	1 c dried, ground figs
½ c warmed honey	2 T chopped orange peel
2 T milk	½ c coconut
2⅔ c flour	

Cream the shortening and sugar; add the eggs and the honey along with the extract. Add the milk, then the dry ingredients, and last the fruit. Drop on a greased cooky sheet, and bake in a moderate oven 10–12 minutes.

These are fine flavored, and healthful as well.

FILLED COOKIES

DOUGH

⅓ c sugar	1½ c flour
⅓ c lard	f.g. salt
1 well-beaten egg	¼ c milk

FILLING

¼ c chopped nuts	1 lb. ground, dried figs
¼ c chopped orange peel	

Mix the lard and sugar; add the egg; then, alternately, the salted flour and milk. Roll thin and cut in large rounds. Place a spoonful of filling, which has been mixed into a stiff paste, on each round. Fold the edges up in sections of four. Pinch the edges, and bake on a greased cooky sheet in a moderate oven 12 minutes.

FRUIT STRIPS

⅓ c shortening	¼ c chopped maraschino
2 c flour	cherries
½ t salt	2 eggs
¼ c sugar	1 egg yolk ⎫
1 t B.P.	1 T water ⎭ mixed, for glaze
½ c ground nuts	

Cut the shortening into the sifted-together, dry ingredients as for piecrust. Add the fruit and nuts, and last the beaten eggs. Pat out to one-half inch thickness on a greased cooky sheet. Brush with the glaze, and sprinkle with G. sugar. Bake in a moderate oven 15 minutes. Cut in strips while still warm.

ITALIAN PASTRY

(1)

1 lb. butter	2 c flour

Mix thoroughly with the hands. Form into a loaf and chill (do not freeze) 20 minutes.

(2)

2 c flour	½ c white wine
3 eggs	

While (1) is chilling, place the flour on a large board. Make a dent in the middle, and drop in the eggs and wine. Using the finger tips, work the eggs and wine into the flour as for noodles. When you have a dough that can be easily handled, roll out thin.

Place the loaf from (1) in the center of this large sheet of dough. Cover it entirely with the dough, and gradually begin to roll, being sure that the dough always covers the butter mixture. Roll thin. Fold in thirds from top to bottom and side to side (like any puff paste). Cover with waxed paper, and chill 20 minutes.

ITALIAN PASTRY

Turn the pastry the opposite way from that in which you finished it. Again roll thin. It will be even more difficult this time, but it can be done. Repeat this rolling and chilling process three times at least. (You are rolling air into it each time, which makes the pastry rise in thin flakes.) After the last rolling, cut in fancy shapes, decorate, and bake in a slow oven 30–40 minutes. Don't bother to grease the pan as the pastry has enough butter in it.

If properly handled, these cookies are like layers of tender flakes. The rolling must be done as quickly as possible and in as cool a room as possible. When finished, handle them as little as possible.

This makes a huge quantity, but the dough may be put in the icebox and kept a week at least, using it only as you need it. In this way you are sure of fresh cookies. These do not keep well because of the great amount of butter used.

Suggested Shapes

(1) The most usual is the large, flat cooky upon which is pressed another of the same size but with a hole cut in the middle as for a doughnut. When these are baked, they will be two inches or more high. Drop a big, preserved strawberry in the hole, and sprinkle with C. sugar.

(2) Roll out in long strips. Put together with honey, icing,

fondant, or any stiff jam. Slice thin, and the cooky will have the appearance of a ribbon if enough strips are put together.

(3) Roll nuts into the dough and make into all sorts of shapes, as crescents, hearts, diamonds, etc.

(4) Cut round cookies, place a preserved fig in the center, then fold the edges over to form a tricorn.

With a set of fancy cutters, and the use of nuts, preserves, colored sugar and candied fruits, there are countless possibilities. The dough itself is not sweet, so the decoration may be.

These are fine for dessert with coffee and *nothing else.* There are so many different sizes and shapes, that the cooky plate will seem to be made up of assorted cakes instead of one variety decorated differently.

Mrs. Josephine DiTirro Baker, Portsmouth, Ohio.

MANTUAN WAFERS

4 c flour	1 lemon rind, grated
½ c sugar	Cold water
¾ c butter	

Mix as for piecrust. Roll thin. Cut in three-inch rounds. On one half of the round, place a teaspoonful of filling. Fold over the other half; pinch the edges together; prick the top. Brush with slightly beaten egg white, and sprinkle with C. sugar. Bake in a moderate oven 10–15 minutes.

FILLING

(1) Stiff jam, marmalade, or preserves.

(2) Stiff custard.

(3) Cottage cheese mixed with sugar, coconut, and spice.

NAPLES CAKES

1 c water	f.g. pepper
¼ c red wine	1 c flour
¼ c white wine	1 egg yolk

Boil the liquids; stir the flour in gradually, and continue to cook slowly until the mass no longer sticks to the pan. Cool 2 minutes. Add the egg yolk. Turn onto a floured board, and knead well. Roll very thin. Cut in shapes, decorate if desired, and bake on a greased cooky sheet in a slow oven until crisp and dry.

They are like a sweet cracker.

SICILIAN RIBBON SLICES

DOUGH

2 c flour	2 egg yolks
¼ c sugar	2 egg whites
2 T shortening	C. sugar

Mix the sugar and shortening. Add the egg yolks and the flour. Roll into long strips, as for noodles. Brush the top of each strip with egg white, and put them together like a long loaf with any or all of the following fillings:

FILLING

(1) B. sugar and cinnamon mixed.

(2) Finely chopped chestnuts or other nuts.

(3) Ground currants mixed with a few drops of lemon juice.

(4) Thick jam or conserve.

Brush the whole loaf with egg white, and decorate the top with citron strips. Bake in a hot oven 20 minutes. Cool and slice as thin as possible. Dust with C. sugar.

These are most attractive and good to the taste.

SIENESE GINGER STRIPS

1 c honey	⅛ t ginger
½ c chopped, unblanched almonds	⅛ lb. grated sweet chocolate
⅛ c chopped peel	1 c rye flour
⅛ t cinnamon	

Warm the honey; add the nuts, peel, spices, and chocolate. Then add the flour. Spread on a greased cooky sheet, and bake in a moderate oven 15 minutes. Cut in strips while still warm, and sprinkle with G. sugar.

These are unusual in flavor—very chewy.

TEA BALLS

½ c shortening	1½ c flour
½ c sugar	¼ t salt
¾ c chopped, unblanched almonds	1 t vanilla
3 eggs	Citron cut in narrow strips

Cream the shortening and sugar; add the eggs, and beat well. Add the rest of the ingredients, and mold into small balls. Roll in C. sugar. Flatten down by pressing into the top a citron strip, first dipped in water or fruit juice to make it stick. Bake in a moderate oven on a greased cooky sheet 10–15 minutes.

These are fine flavored with an ice cream or sherbet, or with tea.

TEA COOKIES

½ c sugar	¼ t vanilla
¼ c butter	¼ t B.P.
½ c flour	1 t water
1 egg yolk	

Cream the butter and sugar; add the egg yolk, water, and vanilla. Beat well. Add the dry ingredients. Roll, using more flour if necessary. Cut. Brush with egg white, and bake in a moderate oven about 10 minutes.

These are quite rich and crisp.

CHINA

VANILLA HORNS
HONEY CANDY SLICES
SESAME SEED COOKIES

Most people think of China, Japan, and rice. Naturally the rice cake is really the cooky of these countries. Other than this and its variations, there is not much which can be called a cooky. There is a rich, candy-like stuff which we have included under cookies because it is so good with tea. All are simple to make, and good to eat.

It must be remembered that the poor in these countries do not have such expensive things as cookies. They are reserved for the well-to-do and the foreigner.

CANDY COOKIES

2 T shortening	1 c B. sugar
⅛ t soda	1½ t water
1 c flour	½ t vanilla

Cream the shortening and sugar. Add the water and vanilla. Add the sifted-together, dry ingredients. Form into balls. Place, two inches apart, on an ungreased cooky sheet, and bake in a moderate oven 20 minutes.

These have much the same flavor as butterscotch candy.

128

DATE SANDWICH COOKIES
DOUGH

1 c chopped dates	½ t B.P.
1 c nuts	f.g. salt
¾ c sugar	2 eggs
¾ c flour	

FILLING

Juice of 1 lemon	½ c coconut

Beat the eggs until light; add the sugar, and beat again. Add the sifted-together, dry ingredients, the nuts, and the dates. Spread thin on a greased, floured cooky sheet. Bake in a moderate oven 20 minutes. Cut in two-inch squares while warm. Squeeze a few drops of lemon juice on one square and sprinkle with coconut, then press another square on top. Cool.

These are rich, and excellent for tea.

HONEY CANDY SLICES

2 c graham cracker crumbs	½ c chopped, preserved or maraschino cherries
1 t almond flavoring	¼ c finely chopped, preserved ginger
1 c finely cut dates	
½ c coconut	¼ c honey
1 c marshmallows, cut fine	

Mix all, adding the cracker crumbs last. Form into long rolls, and chill overnight. Roll in B.sugar and chopped coconut. Slice thin, and bake on a greased cooky sheet in a moderate oven 15 minutes, but watch to prevent burning.

These are very sweet, but tasty with tea.

POPPY SEED COOKIES
DOUGH

1 c butter	3 eggs
2 c sugar	Flour

TOPPING

3 T sugar	2 T poppy seed
1 t vanilla	

Cream the butter; add one cup of sugar, and beat well. Then add the well-beaten eggs, the rest of the sugar, and enough flour to make a dough which will roll. Roll thin. Cut in large rounds and sprinkle with the sugar, poppy seeds, and vanilla mixture. Bake in a moderate oven on a greased cooky sheet 10 minutes or until slightly brown.

RICE WAFERS

¼ c butter	½ c rice flour
½ c C. sugar	⅓ c flour
2 eggs	½ t vanilla
2 T water	¼ t salt

Cream the butter and sugar; add the beaten eggs, the water, and the flavoring. Then add the dry ingredients, sifted together. Spread onto a greased cooky sheet as thin as possible, and bake in a moderate oven about 10 minutes. Cut in large squares.

SESAME SEED COOKIES

1 c butter	3 c flour
2 c sugar	2 t B.P.
2 eggs	½ t salt
½ c water	2 T sesame seeds

Cream the butter and sugar; add the beaten eggs, the water, and the sifted-together, dry ingredients. Sprinkle in the seeds. Chill. Roll thin. Cut, and bake in a moderate oven 15 minutes. These have a special flavor from the sesame seeds.

VANILLA HORNS

1 c butter	1 c flour
2 c sugar	2 t vanilla
3 eggs	

Cream the butter and sugar. Add the beaten egg yolks, the flour, and last the stiffly beaten egg whites and vanilla. Drop at least two inches apart on a greased and floured cooky sheet, and bake in a moderate oven about 10 minutes or until the edges begin to curl. Remove from the oven, but keep the pan on a warm place while you roll each cooky into a small horn. Cool at once so they will keep their shape.

These are unique in appearance, and have the flavor of a most delicious ice-cream cone. They may be eaten plain or filled with flavored whipped cream, but the latter is not at all necessary. They are difficult to make, but worth the effort. If you do not want to attempt the rolling, you may leave them as a large, flat cooky.

WONG'S ALMOND COOKIES

1 c sugar	3 c flour
3/4 c shortening	Almonds for decoration
1/4 t soda	(blanched)
2 T almond flavoring	

Cream the sugar and shortening. Add the soda, flavoring, and flour. Work with the hands until the dough is pliable enough to form small balls. If this becomes too difficult for your powers of perseverance, add 1-2 T water, but only enough to form the dough. Place an almond on top of each ball and bake them on a greased cooky sheet in a moderately slow oven until delicately brown (about 30-40 minutes).

These are rich and gritty, somewhat like Scotch Shortbread. Serve them with a fruit cup, sherbet, or preserved fruits.

Jessie Wong, Cleveland, Ohio.

JAPAN

RICE WAFERS

FRUIT CHEWS

2 eggs	1 c sugar
¾ c flour	1 c chopped nuts
1 t B.P.	1 c chopped dates
¼ t salt	1 c chopped raisins

Mix the dry ingredients; add the fruit, then the well-beaten eggs. Spread thin on a greased, square cake pan, and bake in a moderate oven half an hour. Cut in strips while still warm. Dip in G. sugar.

These are a fine, chewy mouthful.

RICE CAKES

4 egg whites	1 c rice flour
½ c softened butter	1 t vanilla
⅓ c sugar	

Beat the egg whites slightly, and add the sugar and twice-sifted flour, stirring it in very lightly. Fold in the softened butter and vanilla. Drop on a greased cooky sheet at least two inches apart. Spread thin with the back of a floured spoon. Bake in a moderate oven 10 minutes, and they will be crisp and thin.

RICE WAFERS

¼ c butter	2 T water
½ c sugar	½ c rice flour
2 eggs	⅓ c flour

Cream the butter; add the sugar and the unbeaten eggs. Then add the water and the sifted-together, dry ingredients. Flatten out as thin as possible on a greased cooky sheet, and bake in a moderate oven 10 minutes. Cut in squares while still warm.

Anything containing rice flour has a peculiar, almost sandy, texture. These are not rich, but are good served with anything.

TEA WAFERS

1 unbeaten egg white	1 T rice flour
1⅓ T sugar	1½ t soft butter

Mix the ingredients in the order given. Drop, at least two inches apart, on a greased cooky sheet, and bake in a moderate oven about 10 minutes, or until they are light brown around the edge. While still hot, roll into tight rolls, which will remain in shape if they are cooled at once. This amount makes only a few. Double or triple for an ordinary batch.

DENMARK

SHORT BREAD

Scandinavians are all fond of eating. Witness the *Smorgasbord* and the wonderful bread and rolls that are so well known and so good! We haven't heard so much about the cookies, but they do exist, and they are so good. Often they are rich — quite rich, easy to make, but not inexpensive, and worth all that goes into them. The use of hard-cooked eggs is more in vogue here than in any of the other countries. They seem to give a special texture to the dough. Here is a splendid variety which will please all.

DANISH COOKIES

1½ c shortening
1½ c B. sugar
1 egg
1 T orange juice
½ T lemon juice

1 c ground, unblanched
  almonds
½ t cinnamon
3 c flour
¼ t soda

Mix the shortening, sugar, and egg. Beat well and add the juices. When light and foamy, add the sifted-together, dry ingredients and the nuts. Chill three hours, then roll and cut in fancy shapes. Bake in a moderate oven about 10 minutes.

These are rich and very tasty, much like *Dutch Almond Cookies.*

DANISH SHORTBREAD

½ c butter	⅛ t salt
¾ c B. sugar	¾ c chopped nuts
1 egg	½ t B.P.
½ t vanilla	1½–2 c flour

Cream the butter and sugar, add the unbeaten egg, and beat well. Add the vanilla, the sifted-together, dry ingredients, and the nuts. Form little balls (using more flour if necessary), and place on a cooky sheet to bake in a hot oven 8–10 minutes.

This is a cooky which can be made quickly. Coconut may be substituted for the nuts.

ICELAND

EIER KRINGEL

EIER KRINGEL

1 egg	1 lemon rind, grated
3 hard-cooked egg yolks	2 c flour
½ c sugar	½ t powdered cardamon
½ c butter	

Separate the egg and beat the yolk with the mashed, hard-cooked egg yolks, sugar, and butter. Add the dry ingredients, and mix well. Chill one-half hour. Roll thin; cut with doughnut cutter; brush with egg white; sprinkle with G. sugar and finely ground nuts. Bake on a greased cooky sheet in a moderate oven 8-10 minutes. Watch to prevent burning.

At Christmas time these may be very effective if decorated with red and green sugar or red and green candied fruits to imitate a holly wreath.

SPRITZ COOKIES

1 c butter	f.g. salt
¾ c sugar	1 t almond extract
1 egg	2½ c flour
½ t B.P.	

Cream the butter, add the sugar gradually, then the unbeaten egg, and the dry ingredients sifted three times. Add the flavoring. Drop on a greased cooky sheet, or use a cooky press. Decorate as desired. Bake in a moderate oven 5–7 minutes.

NORWAY

MACAROONS

ALMOND COOKIES

½ c ground, blanched almonds	1 egg white
	¼ t cinnamon
⅓ c sugar	½ t grated lemon rind

Beat the egg white stiff. Fold in the almonds, sugar, cinnamon, and lemon rind. Drop by teaspoonfuls on a greased cooky sheet, and bake in a moderate oven 15–20 minutes. Cool.

These will keep a long time and will improve in flavor.

CHRISTMAS WREATHS

½ c butter	2 hard-cooked egg yolks
¼ c sugar	½ t flavoring
1 c flour	

Sieve the eggs, and cream them with the butter. Add the sugar gradually, continuing the creaming. Then add the flour and the flavoring. Roll thin and cut in doughnut-shaped cookies. Decorate with red and green sugar, or cherries to imitate a Christmas wreath. Bake on an ungreased cooky sheet in a moderate oven 8–10 minutes.

COMPANY COOKIES

1½ c butter
1½ c sugar
1 whole egg
1 egg yolk
2½ c flour

1 c finely ground,
  blanched almonds
1 T orange juice
½ t ground cardamon

Pour the butter, melted, over the sugar. Add the eggs and beat until the mixture is foamy. Stir in the almonds, flour, and flavoring. Chill. Roll thin. Cut and bake on a greased cooky sheet in a moderate oven 10 minutes.

KRINGLA

1 c sugar
1 c rich sour cream
½ t salt
¾ t soda

2 t almond or other
  flavoring
3 c flour

Mix the sugar and cream together until all the sugar is dissolved. Add the rest of the ingredients (put the soda in the flour). Drop on a greased cooky sheet, or use a cooky press, and bake in a moderate oven 10 minutes.

MACAROONS

1 c finely ground,
  blanched almonds

½ c C. sugar
½ t egg white

Mix all together, using a little more egg white if necessary to hold the mixture together. Form with the hands into little round cakes. Use C. sugar to keep the mixture from sticking to the hands. Bake in a slow oven on a greased cooky sheet 10–12 minutes. Watch to prevent burning, and remove at once from the pan.

Fine!

NUT COOKIES

½ c butter
½ c sugar
1 c flour

1 egg
½ c chopped,
  unblanched almonds

Cream the butter; then add the sugar, egg, and flour; finally the nuts. With the hands form small balls, denting in the middle of each. Bake on a greased cooky sheet in a moderate oven 20 minutes. When they are done, fill the dent with cream, jam, or marmalade. Omit this if a very sweet cooky is not desired.

TEA COOKIES

1 c sugar	¼ t soda
½ c shortening (½ lard	1 t B.P.
and ½ butter)	⅛ t salt
¼ c sour milk	1 t vanilla
1 egg	2¾ c flour

Cream the shortening; add the sugar, and cream again. Add the unbeaten egg. Stir well. Add the sifted-together, dry ingredients alternately with the milk and vanilla. Chill one hour. Roll very thin. Cut, and bake on a greased cooky sheet in a moderate oven 10 minutes.

These are good plain, but they may be dressed up by decorating with chopped nuts or glazing. They are crisp and good, and quite inexpensive.

TEA DROPS

½ c sugar	½ t cinnamon
½ c sour cream	½ t soda
1½ c flour	½ square chocolate
½ t salt	

Dissolve sugar in cream. Sift dry ingredients and add to first mixture. Melt chocolate and add last. Drop on a greased cooky sheet and bake in a moderate oven for 12 minutes.

SPITZ COOKIES

ALMOND COOKIES

DOUGH

½ c butter
1 c sugar
1 egg

1¾ c flour
1½ t B.P.
½ lemon rind, grated

TOPPING

1 egg
4 T sugar
½ t cinnamon

½ t cloves
Blanched almonds

Cream the butter; add the sugar gradually, then the well-beaten egg. Add the lemon rind and the sifted-together, dry ingredients. Roll very thin, cut in rounds or stars, and brush with egg white. Sprinkle with the spices and sugar mixed, and decorate each cooky with three whole almonds. Bake on a greased cooky sheet in a slow oven 12–15 minutes.

BUTTERSCOTCH OAT COOKIES

1 c quick-cooking oats
⅓ c butter
½ c B. sugar
¼ c finely chopped nuts

1 t B.P.
f.g. salt
1 T sour milk

140

Cream the butter and sugar; add the milk, oats, nuts, salt, and B.P. Mix. Form into balls and place two inches apart on a greased cooky sheet. Bake in a moderate oven 8 minutes or until light brown.

These are really excellent—delightfully crisp.

CHRISTMAS COOKIES

2 hard-cooked egg yolks	1 c flour (more if necessary)
1/3 c butter	1/2 lemon rind, grated
1/3 c sugar	1/2 orange rind, grated
1/3 c heavy sour cream	f.g. salt
1/8 t soda	1 raw egg yolk

TOPPING

1/2 c ground, blanched almonds	5 lumps coarsely crushed sugar
	1 egg white

Rub the mashed eggs with the butter. Add the sugar and mix well. Add the cream, the raw egg yolk, orange, and lemon. Beat together one-half minute. Stir in the sifted-together, dry ingredients. Use enough more flour to make a dough which will roll. Roll thin and cut in star shapes. Brush the top with the egg white; sprinkle with the nuts and sugar. Bake on a greased cooky sheet in a moderately slow oven 15–20 minutes.

GINGER SNAPS

(1)

1/4 c butter	1 t ginger
1/4 c lard	1/8 t nutmeg
1/4 c B. sugar	1/8 t cloves

(2)

1/2 c dark corn syrup, warmed	1 t lemon rind, grated
	1 t lemon juice
1 egg	1/3 c sour cream

(3)

2 t B.P.	1/4 t salt
1/4 t soda	3 c flour

Mix 1 and 2, then add 3 all sifted together. Let stand overnight in a cool place. Roll out thin; cut; and bake only 5 minutes in a moderate oven.

If a decorated cooky is desired, use fruit or nut decoration before baking; however, they really need no "dressing up." Do not confuse these with the American type, which is darker and more spicy.

MACAROONS

1 c finely ground nuts	1 egg
¼ c cornstarch	1 orange rind, grated
1 c sugar	

Mix the sugar and egg. Add the orange, the cornstarch, and the nuts. With floured hands, form the dough into small balls. Bake 2 inches apart on a greased cooky sheet in a slow oven 10–15 minutes.

NUT COOKIES

½ c butter	2 t B.P.
½ c sugar	½ c finely chopped nuts
1 c rye flour	½ c chopped raisins
1 c white flour	4 T milk

Cream the butter and sugar. Add the nuts and raisins. Add the milk and the sifted-together, dry ingredients alternately. Roll thin and cut. Bake on a greased cooky sheet in a moderate oven 15 minutes.

RYE WAFERS

⅔ c butter	2 c rye flour
½ c C. sugar	2 T water
⅛ t B.P.	

Cream the butter and sugar. Add the rest of the ingredients. Roll thin and cut. Bake in a slow oven, on a greased cooky sheet, 20 minutes.

These have an unusual flavor due to the rye flour.

SAND STRIPS

⅔ c butter
⅔ c C. sugar
1 egg
2 T thin cream

½ t almond extract
2 c flour
2 t B.P.

Mix in the order given to form a soft dough. Press onto a greased cooky sheet as thin as possible. Bake in a hot oven 8 minutes. When slightly cool, cut in finger lengths and decorate with any glaze. They may also be decorated with nuts before baking, but they are quite good without them.

SAND TARTS

2 c sugar
1 c butter
½ c lard

2 eggs
3 c flour
½ t almond extract

Mix the butter and lard, and the sugar. Add the unbeaten eggs, the flour, and the flavoring. Form into balls and bake, two inches apart, on a greased cooky sheet in a slow oven 10 minutes.

SPITZ COOKIES

⅓ c butter
½ c C. sugar
1 egg yolk

1 c flour
⅛ t salt
½ t almond extract

Mix in the order given. Chill one-half hour. Form into "S" shapes, using the hands or a cooky press. Brush with egg white. Bake on a greased cooky sheet in a hot oven 8 minutes.

SWEDES

1¾ c C. sugar
1 c chopped almonds
1 c flour
1 egg

1 egg white
1 vanilla bean, ground
and sifted

Mix all, and form small round balls. Dust with C. sugar, and bake on a greased cooky sheet in a moderate oven until straw colored.

"U" COOKIES

¼ c shortening	1⅓ c flour
¾ c sugar	¼ t salt
1 egg	1 t vanilla
2 T milk	1½ t B.P.

Cream the shortening; add the sugar and the beaten egg. Add the vanilla and the milk, then the sifted-together, dry ingredients. Spread thin on a greased, square cake pan, and bake in a moderate oven 10 minutes. Remove from the oven, but keep in a warm place while cutting in long strips. Wrap each strip around a broom handle to form the "U" which will retain its shape if the cookies are cooled at once.

These add a novelty element to the cooky assortment.

MJUK PEPPAR KAKOR (Christmas Cookies)

1 c butter	2 t soda
1½ c sugar	1 T cinnamon
3 T white syrup	1 T ginger
2 eggs	1 T cloves
3 c flour	

Cream the butter and sugar. Add the syrup and eggs. Add the sifted-together, dry ingredients. Work into a stiff dough. Roll very thin on a floured board. Cut into shapes and bake in a moderate oven about 10 minutes.

These are an excellent, crisp cooky for any time of the year. At Christmas, they should be cut and decorated in keeping with the season.

Mrs. Elsa Håkonnsson Hosack, Plumwood, Gates Mills, Ohio.

SCOTLAND

SCOTCH FANCIES
EDINBURGH TEA FINGERS

"The Land o' Cakes," somebody has called it, and somebody was right. The bakeshops are full of the most alluring things—all crumbly, rich, nutty, and fragrant. Here is rolled oats, which you'll like regardless of what your private opinion of porridge may be. Here are buns, rich as any fruit cake; here, also, is the famous *Shortbread* which even the poor have at times, usually Christmas. They're good, they're rich, and they're easy to make; and whoever eats them wants another serving. You'd better make a large quantity.

ABERNETHY BISCUITS

6 T butter	1 t caraway seed (other,
6 T sugar	if preferred)
2 c flour	1 egg
½ t B.P.	1 T milk

Rub the butter into the flour; add the sugar, B.P., and seeds. Beat the egg and add it to the milk. Add this mixture to the first mixture. Roll little balls with the hands and flatten them out on a cooky sheet. Bake in a moderate oven 10 minutes.

These are like a shortbread, but less rich.

Roberta Abernethy, Columbus, Ohio.

AUNT MARY'S OATMEAL COOKIES

1¼ c sugar	1 lb. dates, seeded and
1 c lard	cut fine (2 c)
3 c rolled oats	1 t soda
2 eggs	2 c flour
½ c sour milk	1 t salt
2 t ginger	

Cream the sugar and lard; add the eggs, the sour milk, and the sifted-together, dry ingredients. Add the dates and the oats. Form into little balls with the hands. Bake on a greased cooky sheet in a moderate oven 15 minutes.

Raisins may be substituted for the dates. This makes a big "batch."

BLACK BUN COOKIES
DOUGH

2 c flour	⅓ c sugar
½ t B.P.	2 T water
½ c butter	

FILLING

¼ c flour	½ c raisins
¼ c sugar	½ c currants
¼ c milk	¼ c candied peel
¼ t soda	¼ c citron
¼ t cinnamon	¼ c chopped nuts
¼ t ginger	

Mix the butter and sugar. Add the water, then the dry ingredients. Roll thin. Cut in rounds. Put a spoonful of the filling on each round. Moisten the edges with water and put another round on top. Pinch the edges together and prick the tops. Bake on a greased cooky sheet in a moderate oven 16 minutes or until brown on top.

BUTTERSCOTCH BARS

½ c B. sugar	½ t B.P.
⅛ t salt	½ c chopped nuts
1 egg	¾ c flour

Mix the sugar, salt and egg, and beat one minute. Add the dry ingredients and the nuts. Spread thin on a greased, square cake pan, and bake in a moderate oven 20 minutes. When slightly cool, cut in bars. Remove and sprinkle with C. sugar.

These are butterscotchy and chewy, just the thing to crunch on while you read, provided everybody crunches at the same time.

COPELAND MATTIES

Use the Scotch Shortbread recipe No. 1 and add ½ c ground, unblanched almonds and ¼ c finely cut citron. Make into round cakes three inches across and one-half inch thick. Pinch the edges as for piecrust. Bake in a slow oven until they are a delicate brown.

DOUGLAS MAC ARTHUR STRIPS

½ c shortening	¼ c sherry or fruit juice
½ c C. sugar	(light color for a
2 eggs	light-colored cooky)
¼ c chopped nuts	1 c flour
1 lemon rind, grated	½ t B.P.
½ c chopped peel	½ t cinnamon and cloves
	mixed

Cream the shortening and sugar, and the beaten eggs. Add the lemon rind, nuts, peel, and sherry. Add the sifted-together, dry ingredients. Spread one-half inch thick on a greased cooky sheet, and bake in a moderate oven 15 minutes. Cool and cut in long strips. Dust with C. sugar.

EDINBURGH TEA FINGERS

DOUGH

¾ c butter	2 c rolled oats
1 c sugar	½ t salt
1 c flour	

FILLING

1 c water	1½ c chopped dates (or
1 T lemon juice	raisins, figs, or currants)

Cook the filling until a paste is formed. Watch that it does not burn. Cream the butter; stir in the sugar, the sifted-together, dry ingredients, and the oats. Work with the hands to form a crumbly dough, one half of which is to be forced onto a greased, square cake pan in a thin layer. Cover this with the filling, and spread the remainder of the dough (don't be alarmed if it seems very crumbly) on top. Bake in a slow oven 30 minutes. If a very crunchy cooky is desired, use steel-cut oats instead of rolled oats. Cut in fingers while still warm. Remove carefully from the pan.

These are rich and tasty, and should be used soon after baking.

FANS

1 c butter	½ t salt
1 c B. sugar	¼ t soda
2½ c flour (more, if	1 t B.P.
needed)	1 egg

Cream the butter and sugar. Add the beaten egg, and mix well. Add the sifted-together, dry ingredients. Roll thin (use more flour to make the dough handle easily). Cut in large, round cookies with a fluted cooky cutter; then cut these into fan shapes. Mark with a knife as for a fan. Bake on a greased cooky sheet in a slow oven 15–20 minutes.

HONEY CAKES

¼ c sugar	1 t cinnamon
½ c honey	½ t ginger
¼ c chopped citron	1½ c flour
¼ c chopped orange peel	

Heat the honey and the sugar. Add the rest of the ingredients. This will form a very stiff dough. Flatten it down on a greased cooky sheet, and bake in a moderate oven 12 minutes. Remove from the oven. Mark in squares or triangles while still warm. Cool.

They improve in flavor and texture with age.

HONEY FINGERS

2 c rolled oats	¼ c milk
(quick cook)	¼ c honey
½ t salt	1½ T melted butter
¼ c sugar	1 egg
2 t B.P.	½ c flour

Mix the oats, flour, sugar, salt, and B.P. Add the milk to the beaten egg. Warm the honey, and add to the milk-egg mixture. Mix all well and add the butter. Bake in a thin layer on a greased cooky sheet in a slow oven 25 minutes. When slightly cool, cut in long, finger-like strips.

OAT SQUARES

2 c rolled oats	2 t B.P.
(quick cook)	¼ c milk
½ t salt	¼ c light corn syrup
¼ c B. sugar	1½ T melted butter

Grind the rolled oats; mix in the salt, B.P., sugar, and milk. Then add the syrup and butter. Mix well. Roll thin, and cut in squares. Bake on a greased cooky sheet in a slow oven 20 minutes.

These are much like *Honey Fingers*, but less rich and interesting to look at.

SAM'S FAVORITE BUTTERSCOTCHIES

½ c shortening (at least	2 c flour
½ butter)	¼ t soda
1 c B. sugar	½ t B.P.
½ t vanilla	⅛ t salt
1 egg	½ c chopped nuts

Mix in the order given, and work into a long roll. Chill overnight. Slice very thin, and bake on a greased cooky sheet in a moderate oven 5–8 minutes.

These are very crisp and "flavorful."

SCOTCH SHORTBREAD No. 1

1 c flour
½ c rice flour
¾ c butter

½ c sugar
½ c blanched almond
strips

Sift the flour twice, and rub in the butter with the hands. Add the sugar, and work until a dough is formed. Make into a long roll. Chill well. Slice thin and decorate with the almond strips. Bake on an ungreased cooky sheet, in a moderate oven, until golden brown.

This is a good recipe, much liked by Americans. The rice flour intensifies the texture, but other flour may be used if it is not available.

SCOTCH SHORTBREAD No. 2

2 lb. flour (8 c)
1 lb. C. sugar (3⅔ c)

1 lb. butter (2 c)

Work the butter with the hands until it is soft and creamy. Add the sugar gradually, then the flour in the same manner, continuing to work and knead until a well-blended dough is formed. This will take a long time, but don't be discouraged as the result justifies the labor. Press the dough ⅝ inch thick on round pans. With a fork prick a design on the top, or make a real Scotch decoration by pressing the side of your thumbnail around the edge, as for piecrust. Make several cuts, about an inch long, through to the bottom of the pan to let the air escape and prevent the *Shortbread* from puffing in the middle. Bake in a slow oven until a very delicate brown. This will keep several weeks if packed in tins. It may be made up in small cookies, but the large *Shortbread* is more truly Scotch. This recipe makes a great amount of *Short-bread*. For an ordinary family one half or one fourth of the recipe would be sufficient.

It should be broken in small pieces and served with a hot beverage, such as tea; or a cold beverage, such as wine. It is well to keep it on hand at holiday time.

This recipe has been used in the MacCall family for generations. It was brought to Canada, and then to the United States, by Mr. MacCall's father, Mr. Alexander MacCall, Sr., who was a baker in Scotland. It is the custom for the head of the family to make the *Shortbread* at Christmas time, a rite of which he is very proud.

Alexander MacCall, Cleveland, Ohio.

SCOTCH SHORTBREAD No. 3
"Real Scotch Shortcake"

1 lb. butter (2 c)	5 c flour (perhaps more)
1 c B. or G. sugar	

Knead the butter and sugar together. Work in the flour grad-ually till there is enough to form a good, smooth dough. Divide the dough in three parts, then flatten each of these parts, one-half inch thick, onto a pie plate. Bake in a moderate oven until golden brown. Sprinkle with C. sugar when they come from the oven. Cut while still warm, and serve.

"You can put a fancy stitch around the edge and a leaf orna-ment in the middle, or decorate as you like."

Mrs. Russell Squire, Chillicothe, Ohio.

NOTE.—There seem to be a great many ideas as to just what is the "real Scotch shortbread." Each Scot will tell you a different thing according to what has been customary in his family. At least it is a very well-known and popular dish of Scotland, and we give you three different versions of "the real thing" so that you may take what pleases you

SCOTTISH FANCIES

½ c sugar	1 egg
⅔ T melted butter	⅓ t salt
⅔ c rolled oats	¼ t vanilla
(quick cook)	¼ c nuts (if desired)
⅓ c coconut	

Add the sugar gradually to the beaten egg, then add the rest of the ingredients. Drop on a greased, floured cooky sheet, and bake in a hot oven 5 minutes, after which lower the fire and bake in a slow oven 15 minutes more.

These are very easy to make, are inexpensive, and still as good and attractive as a macaroon.

SUGAR COOKIES

½ c butter	1 t B.P.
1 c sugar	2 c flour
¼ c milk	½ t cinnamon
1 egg	1 t vanilla

Cream the butter and sugar; add the unbeaten egg and vanilla, and beat well. Add the sifted-together, dry ingredients alternately with the milk. Use more flour, if needed, to roll. Cut and sprinkle with sugar, or brush with white of egg and sugar. Bake in a hot oven 10 minutes or until brown on top.

TOASTED OATMEAL WAFERS

½ c butter	¼ t salt
¾ c B. sugar	1½ c flour
2 eggs	3 t B.P.
¾ c toasted oatmeal	1 t cinnamon
(let it dry and toast	¼ c currants or raisins
in a slow oven)	

Cream the butter and sugar. Add the eggs and the dry ingredients to which the currants have been added. Form into a long roll, and chill overnight. Slice thin, and bake in a moderate oven 10 minutes.

These are very crisp and have a special flavor coming from the toasted oats.

SWITZERLAND

COCONUT BALLS

It is to be expected that the cookery of the Swiss people will show many likenesses to the Italian, German, French, and Austrian, since these countries surround Switzerland, which is comparatively small in area. The *Peppernut* and the *Fruit Cookies* are like those of Germany; there is a *Springerle* recipe so near like the German that it has not been included in this book. Some of these will seem like the French *Petits Fours,* and some like a rich Austrian cooky; but in every case the Swiss people have made the recipes their own. They are known as good cooks throughout the world for they have the "magic touch." Their cookies prove this.

The poor people do not often have cookies except at Christmas time, when it is the custom for them to celebrate with some sweet cakes, sweet breads, and cookies, which they use first for tree decoration and then for their stomachs. The wealthy, of course, have theirs much more often than once a year.

BASLER LEKERLI (Bazil Sweets)

2 c honey
2 c sugar
5 c ground, unblanched
    almonds
¼ c rum, brandy, or
    fruit juice
1 orange rind, grated

1 lemon rind, grated
1 t cloves
1 t cinnamon
½ t nutmeg
1 c citron, ground
7 c flour

BASLER LEKERLI

Melt the honey and add the other ingredients. Let this chill for a week. When ready to bake, warm the dough and roll into a sheet. Cut and bake in a moderate oven, on a greased cooky sheet, 10 minutes. While still warm, take from the pan and glaze. (See p. 174.)

These keep a long time in cooky jar; and this makes a huge amount. Cut it down for the average family.

Mrs. H. Brinkman, Westerville, Ohio.

COCONUT BALLS

4 egg whites
1 c C. sugar
2 c coconut

½ c flour
1 t vanilla

Beat the egg whites stiff; add the vanilla and the sugar gradually. Add the flour and the coconut. Drop, an inch apart, on a greased and floured cooky sheet. Bake in a moderate oven 15 minutes.

Excellent!

Mrs. Ruth Schneider, Westerville, Ohio.

YULETIDE KISSES

4 egg whites	Cinnamon candies, angelica,
f.g. salt	or chocolate shot for
1 c chopped walnuts	decoration
1 c sugar	

Beat the egg whites and the salt until very stiff and dry. Add the sugar gradually and then the nuts. Decorate with any one of the suggested things. Drop an inch apart on a greased and floured cooky sheet, and bake in a slow oven 25 minutes.

These are good and attractive.

YULETIDE STRIPS

1 c sugar	2 egg yolks
1 c butter	2¼ c flour

Cream the sugar and butter. Add the eggs and flour. Pat the dough into two square, greased baking pans with sides. Bake in a slow oven for 20 minutes. Remove from the oven. Cover with Topping and bake for 30 minutes more in a slow oven. Cut into strips and roll while still warm in C. sugar.

TOPPING

2 egg whites	1¼ c sugar
4 whole eggs	1 t vanilla
2 c finely cut nuts	
(Black walnuts are es-	
pecially delicious)	

Beat the egg whites until foamy. Add the beaten eggs and the rest of the ingredients.

These are rich and unusual and not as difficult to make as they seem. Serve them with the Christmas cooky assortment or as a good desert for any meal.

Mrs. Haven L. Zebold, Cleveland, Ohio.

Miscellaneous

AUSTRALIA, BELGIUM, BOHEMIA, GREECE, POLAND,
RUSSIA, SPAIN, TURKEY, WALES AND WEST INDIES

Many of these countries are represented by only a few recipes because either they do not pay much attention to this side of the menu, or we have been unable to secure any representative recipes, or the recipes are so very much like those of other countries by which they are bounded or to which they are closely related. Australia and Wales have naturally borrowed from England. Russia has imitated France. We have, therefore, included all these under one general heading with the appropriate subdivisions according to countries.

Australia

AUSTRALIAN LADY FINGERS

1½ c flour	½ t B.P.
1 c sugar	1 t pineapple flavoring
3 eggs	

Beat the eggs and sugar two minutes. Let stand half an hour Stir in the flour and B.P., then beat half a minute. Add the flavoring. Bake in a greased, square cake pan in a moderate oven until slightly brown on top and shrinking from the sides of the pan. Cut in long fingers, and sprinkle with C. sugar.

Any flavor may be substituted for the pineapple.

CHOCOLATE SQUARES

½ c butter	1 egg
¼ c sugar	1 lemon rind, grated
1 c flour	1 square chocolate, grated

158

Cream the butter and sugar; stir in the egg yolk, chocolate, and lemon. Add the flour. Beat well. Fold in the stiffly beaten egg white. Pour into a greased, square cake pan, an inch thick. Bake in a moderate oven 20 minutes. Cut in squares when almost cool, and sprinkle with C. sugar.

Belgium

BELGIAN NEW YEAR CAKES (Galettes)

1 lb. butter (2 c)	1 lb. flour (4 c)
1 lb. sugar (2 c)	8 eggs

Melt the butter. Add the sugar, the flour, and last the eggs. Mix well. Add flavoring if desired. Bake on a waffle or galette iron. Cut in small cookies.

These keep well, and are very fine served with tea.

Mrs. Dorothy Criswell Price, Evergreen Farm, Newark, Ohio.

CHOCOLATE MACAROONS

½ c salad oil or melted shortening	4 eggs
4 squares of melted, bitter chocolate	2 t vanilla
2 c sugar	2 c flour
	2 t B.P.

Combine the first three ingredients. Add the eggs one at a time and beat all after each addition. Add the vanilla and then the sifted-together, dry ingredients. Chill well. With the hands form small balls. Drop them in C. sugar. Bake on a greased cooky sheet two inches apart in a moderate oven 12–15 minutes.

These are excellent in flavor and most attractive.

Mrs. John Richardson, Shaker Heights, Ohio.

BOHEMIA

DIAMOND COOKIES

DIAMOND COOKIES

3 T heavy sweet cream	2 eggs
2 T sugar	1¾ c flour

Beat the eggs until light and add the sugar, cream, and flour. Roll very thin and cut in diamonds. Brush the tops with cream and place on a heavily greased cooky sheet. Bake in a moderate oven about 5 minutes. Sprinkle with C. sugar and cinnamon as soon as they come from the oven.

These are much like a sweet cracker. Originally they were fried in deep fat, but the baking method is easier.

HOLIDAY COOKIES

1 egg yolk (hard-cooked and mashed)	½ T milk
	½ lemon rind, grated
1¼ c butter	2 c flour
3 T sugar	¼ c nuts (for top)
1 raw egg yolk (save white for brushing)	

160

Mix in the order given and chill one-half hour. Roll and cut in fancy shapes. Brush with egg white slightly beaten and diluted with 1 t water. Sprinkle with G. sugar and nuts. Bake on an ungreased cooky sheet in a hot oven 5 minutes.

These are very rich, but appropriate for holidays.

MORAVIAN COOKIES

1 c sugar	½ t cinnamon
½ c butter	½ t nutmeg
2 c flour	1 T brandy or fruit juice
2 eggs	1 t soda

Cream the butter and sugar; add the unbeaten eggs, and beat well. Add the brandy and the sifted-together, dry ingredients. Roll thin. Cut and bake on a greased cooky sheet in a moderate oven until brown.

These can be made as icebox cookies.

Greece

CANDY COOKIES

1 c flour	¼ c walnuts or
¼ c whole wheat flour	chopped almonds
¼ c sugar	¼ c mixed hard candy,
⅛ c chopped raisins	finely broken
	5 T rose water

Mix in the order given. If a wafer-like cooky is desired, roll thin, cut, and bake on a greased cooky sheet in a moderate oven 5–8 minutes. Small balls may be made and baked in the same way.

NUT WAFERS

⅛ c raisins	1 c flour
¼ c hazelnuts	¾ c sugar
½ c walnuts	¼ c rose water
⅛ c almonds	¼ t cinnamon
⅛ c pistachio nuts	

Grind the nuts and raisins. Mix all the ingredients well. Roll thin, cut, and bake on a greased cooky sheet in a moderate oven

10 minutes. If the rose water is not liked, use any fruit juice. If all the varieties of nuts are not available, use ¾ c of any one variety, but the flavor will not be quite the same.

SUGAR COOKIES

½ c butter	¼ c sugar
2 c flour	

Melt the butter, but do not let it boil. Add this to the flour and sugar, working and kneading it in. If the mixture is too dry, add a few drops of water. Work for five minutes. Then roll as thin as possible (this seems impossible, but it can be done). Cut, sprinkle with sugar, and bake in a slow oven 10 minutes. Watch as they burn easily.

These are like a shortbread, and they improve with age.

Poland

POLISH WAFERS

⅓ c sugar	1 egg
3 T butter	2 c flour
2 T fruit juice or brandy	f.g. salt

Cream the butter and sugar, and add the unbeaten egg and salt. Beat well, then add the brandy. Mix in the flour, using more, if needed, for rolling. Cut. Prick with a fork as for a cracker. Bake on a greased cooky sheet in a moderate oven 8 minutes, and watch to prevent burning.

These are very much like a sweet cracker.

RUSSIA

TEA COOKIES

DROP COOKIES

½ c butter	1 c raisins
¾ c B. sugar	1 c chopped pecans
2 c flour	1 t soda
1 egg	½ c boiling water
½ t each, cinnamon, allspice, and cloves	

Cream the butter and sugar, add the unbeaten egg, and beat well. Add the spices, raisins, nuts, and soda mixed with the water. Stir in the flour. Drop on a greased cooky sheet, and bake in a moderate oven 10 minutes. Decorate the top with a nut before baking.

TEA COOKIES

1 c sugar	¾ c butter
3 eggs	½ t B.P.
1 c sour cream	½ t salt
4–5 c flour (enough to roll)	Sugar and cinnamon (for top)
1 c chopped almonds	

163

Mix the sugar, slightly beaten eggs, sour cream, flour, B.P., and salt. Toss on a floured board. Spread with a layer of butter. Roll up as for jelly roll. Place dough in a bowl. Cover and chill (do not freeze) one-half hour. Roll as thin as possible. Strew with chopped almonds, sugar, and cinnamon. Roll like a jelly roll, and cut in fourth-inch rounds. Bake on a greased cooky sheet in a moderately hot oven 10–12 minutes.

This is like a puff paste dough.

TRIANGLES

6 eggs	1 T caraway seeds
1 c sugar	1/4 t salt
1½ c flour	1 t vanilla

Beat the egg yolks until lemon colored. Stir in the sugar, salt, and vanilla. Sift the flour three times and sprinkle the seeds into it. Add the flour gradually to the egg mixture, and fold in the stiffly beaten egg whites. Pour into a greased, square cake pan, and bake in a hot oven about 10 minutes. Cut in triangles and return to the oven (slow) 5 minutes, to dry out.

Spain

SPANISH CINNAMON CRACK

2 c flour	1/4 t salt
2 t cinnamon	

Mix and add enough water to form a smooth dough. Knead and slap into long strips three inches wide. Cut into wafer-like sticks. Bake on a greased cooky sheet in a slow oven about 30 minutes.

They should be very crisp and thin, and are fine served just that way or iced with *Mocha Glaze*, page 174. They improve with age, and are good served with any rich dessert since they are not rich in themselves. They go well with wine and any other beverage.

LITTLE ORANGE DROPS

1 c water	3 eggs
½ c butter	1 orange rind, grated
¼ c sugar	f.g. salt
1¼ c flour	⅓ c chopped almonds

Bring sugar, salt, butter, and water to a boil. Remove from the fire and add the flour all at once. Stir well. Add the unbeaten eggs, beating each one in thoroughly before the next one is added. Add the orange rind. Drop in very small drops on a greased cooky sheet. Brush with beaten egg white, and sprinkle with almonds mixed with a little C. sugar. Bake in a hot oven 10 minutes, then a moderate oven 15–20 minutes more or until they are straw colored and dried out inside.

They may be filled with sweetened, flavored whipped cream or some sweetened fruit, but they must be used soon after they are baked. They are very good without any filling.

SPICE SQUARES

DOUGH

½ c butter	2 t B.P.
1 c sugar	1 t cinnamon
2 eggs	½ t nutmeg
½ c milk	½ t cloves
1¾ c flour	

TOPPING

¾ c currants	Cinnamon
3 T G. sugar	

Cream the butter, sugar, and egg yolks. Add the milk and the sifted-together, dry ingredients. Fold in the stiffly beaten egg whites. Spread on a greased cooky sheet one inch thick. Strew the top with sugar, cinnamon, and currants. Bake in a moderate oven 20 minutes. Cut in two-inch squares.

These are delicious, but must be eaten fresh, as they soon dry out.

TURKEY

SANDWICH COOKIES

TURKISH FINGERS

DOUGH

¾ c sugar   2 c flour
¼ c butter   ½ t B.P.
2 eggs

FILLING

Melted butter   1 c finely chopped nuts
½ c sugar

Cream the butter and the sugar. Add the eggs, and beat well. Add B.P. to flour, then sift all into the first mixture. Chill one hour. Take one half of the dough and roll thin. Place it on the cooky sheet. Brush with melted butter and sprinkle thickly with the chopped nuts mixed with the sugar. Roll out the other half of the dough and place it over the first, pressing the edges slightly together. Brush it with melted butter, then sprinkle with a little more of the sugar. Bake on a greased cooky sheet in a moderate oven until brown. Cool slightly and cut into long, finger-like cookies.

SANDWICH COOKIES

DOUGH

¼ c butter
⅔ c sugar
1 egg
1 c flour
½ t B.P.
f.g. salt
¼ t soda

½ t cinnamon
½ t nutmeg
3 T sour milk or buttermilk
6 dates, chopped fine
¼ c nuts, chopped fine
⅓ c thick jam

Cream the butter and sugar. Add the beaten egg, sour milk, and sifted-together, dry ingredients. Then add the dates, nuts, and jam. Spread one-third inch thick on a greased cake pan, and bake in a moderate oven 15 minutes. Cut the layer in half, and put together as a sandwich with the filling. Then cut in long-finger strips.

FILLING

⅓ c C. sugar
1 t coffee

⅓ t vanilla
1 t cream

WALES

BAKESTONE CAKES

BAKESTONE CAKE

2½ c flour
4 T lard
2½ t B.P.
1 c sugar (scant)
1 t nutmeg

1 c currants or seedless
  raisins
2 T minced lemon peel
1 c milk

Rub the lard in the sifted-together, dry ingredients, and add the milk, currants, and lemon peel. Roll thin and cut round. Bake on a greased cooky sheet in a moderate oven 15 minutes. Split open and butter for afternoon tea, if you like, but they are rich and delicious just as they are.

If you want to be really old-fashioned and do this as our grandmothers did, bake the cakes on a griddle, turning them as pancakes.

West Indies

WEST INDIAN GINGER COOKIES

1 c molasses	¼ c preserved ginger syrup
¼ c B. sugar	4 c flour
½ c preserved ginger, chopped fine	1 c C. sugar (for dusting the cookies after baking)

Boil molasses, sugar, ginger, and syrup one minute. Add the flour and enough more to make a dough that will roll. Roll thin, cut, and bake on a greased cooky sheet in a moderate oven 10–12 minutes. These may be made as ice-box cookies. In any case, do not use too much extra flour or they will be tough instead of crisp.

These are unusual because of the preserved ginger. Very snappy.

FRESH COCONUT CAKES

2 egg whites	½ c sugar
f.g. salt	2 c grated, fresh coconut

Beat the egg whites and salt until stiff. Gradually add the sugar, beating all the while. Fold in the coconut and bake in small drops on a greased cooky sheet in a moderate oven 10–15 minutes, but watch to prevent burning.

Cooky Decorations

I. *Frostings*. —Sometimes called icings, they are like those used for cakes. Suggestions are given here in order to save time, but in any case your own "pet recipe" may be substituted.

CHOCOLATE CREAM ICING

1 c sugar	½ c coffee cream
2 T cocoa	½ t vanilla

Mix the sugar and cocoa, and add the cream. Cook slowly to the soft-ball stage (234° F.), stirring frequently. Beat until creamy and thick enough to spread. Add the vanilla.

DECORATING FROSTING

2½ c sugar	½ t vanilla
½ c light corn syrup	2 egg whites
½ c water	

Cook the sugar, syrup, and water until it spins a thread. Pour the syrup slowly on the stiffly beaten egg whites. Beat well; add the vanilla, and when thick enough to spread, put a thin layer on the cooky. Let it dry and decorate with the remainder, which is stiff enough to hold its shape and may be pushed through a pastry tube. This will keep in a covered jar in the icebox for several days, and may be used as desired.

DIVINITY FROSTING

2½ c sugar	2 egg whites
⅔ c water	½ t vanilla
⅓ c light corn syrup	

In a large, covered pan, cook the syrup, sugar, and water until it spins a thread. Pour it slowly over the stiffly beaten egg whites, add the vanilla; then beat until the mass is very stiff. If it becomes too stiff to spread, add a few drops of water. For a darker frosting, use dark corn syrup.

EIGHT-MINUTE CARAMEL FROSTING

1 c B. sugar	1 egg white
3 T water	½ t vanilla

Stir the sugar and water until the sugar is dissolved; add the egg white, and beat over boiling water 8 minutes. Add the vanilla, and spread.

FLUFFY FROSTING

2 egg whites	5 T cold water
1½ c sugar	½ t vanilla

Place the egg whites in the upper part of a double boiler; beat until stiff and add the sugar and water. Set over boiling water, and place over a low fire. Beat with the rotary egg beater until the icing stands in peaks (this requires from 7–10 minutes). Add the vanilla, and beat until cold.

FLUFFY CONFECTIONER'S SUGAR FROSTING

1 egg white	¼ t cream of tartar
1½ T cold water	½ t flavoring

Beat all two minutes and add confectioner's sugar, beating after each addition until the mixture is of the right consistency to spread. It should be smooth and fluffy, and may be colored if desired.

FONDANT FROSTING

2 c sugar	¼ t cream of tartar
½ c cold water	

Mix all the ingredients in a pan so large that they will not boil over. Cover and boil until the soft-ball stage is reached, testing at intervals. Pour on a platter dampened with water, and let it cool until a dent can be made on the surface. Then work back and forth with a spoon until a creamy mass is produced. Work with the hands, forming a ball which is to be placed in a bowl and covered with a dampened cloth and waxed paper. Allow to stand twenty-four hours. When ready to use, place the desired amount in the top of a double boiler, and heat until it is the consistency to spread.

This is a good frosting for most small cookies. Any flavoring or coloring may be added. A list of suggestions follows, and others may be added according to personal preference:

1. Almond . . . . ½ t almond extract
2. Black walnut . . . . ½ t extract
3. Butter . . . . 1 t butter
4. Candies or shot may be sprinkled on top
5. Candied peel or nuts may be placed on top
6. Chocolate . . . . ½ t vanilla and sprinkle top
   with grated chocolate
7. Coconut . . . . ½ t vanilla and sprinkle top
   with coconut
8. Lemon . . . . ½ t lemon extract
9. Maple . . . . ½ t maplene or maple syrup
10. Peppermint . . . . few drops of the essence
11. Pineapple . . . . ½ t extract
12. Pistachio . . . . ¼ t extract
13. Vanilla . . . . 1 t extract

PENUCHE OR CARAMEL FROSTING

2 c B. sugar   2 T butter
½ c milk   ½ t vanilla

Cook the sugar and milk until the soft-ball stage is reached, stirring frequently. Add the butter, and beat until creamy; then the vanilla. If the frosting becomes too hard, add a few drops of milk. Cream may be substituted for the milk, and the butter may be omitted, if a finer-grained product is desired.

UNCOOKED MOCHA FROSTING

2 c C. sugar   ½ t vanilla
6 T butter   Strong coffee
4 T cocoa

Cream the butter, sugar, and cocoa. Add enough hot, strong coffee to make a creamy mixture which will spread easily. Blend well, and add the vanilla.

This is a very simple type of frosting, and particularly good for the beginner who is afraid that all frosting will "go to sugar." It admits of endless variation if the cocoa, vanilla, and coffee are omitted and the liquid changed.

Fruit.—Use 1 T boiling water, grated orange or lemon rind, and enough of any fruit juice, such as lemon, orange, pineapple, etc., to make a creamy mass.

Liquors.—Brandy, wine, etc., and the 1 T of boiling water give a pleasant flavor for those who like it.

II. *Glazes.*—Cookies may be glazed (given a shiny appearance) before or after baking. Simply spread the cooky with a thin layer of glaze.

A. Before Baking

1. One egg white diluted with 1 T water
2. One egg yolk mixed with 1 T water
3. Milk or cream
4. Fruit and nuts placed on the glazed surface

B. After Baking

1. Confectioner's Sugar Glaze
   ¾ c C. sugar
   1 T hot liquid (more if necessary)
   1 square chocolate (for chocolate glaze)

   Mix and spread on the cooky. Variations may be secured by changing the liquid. Any fruit juice, butter, cream, evaporated milk, coffee, or commercial extracts may be used.

2. *Marshmallow.*—Place on top of a plain cooky a piece of marshmallow. Allow it to brown slightly and eat at once as it will not save.

III. *Fruit and Nut Decorations.*—This must be done before the cooky is baked, and it is an excellent way to "dress up" a cooky. Arrange on each cooky such things as whole or finely chopped nut meats, candied peel, raisins, currants, coconut, plain and colored sugar, or slices of fruits, such as figs, prunes, and apricots. If the dough is not moist enough to hold the decoration, put a drop of water, honey, or syrup where the decoration is to be.

MAKE THESE IF YOU HAVE

Sour Cream

Sour Milk or Buttermilk

INDEX

A CATALOGUE OF SELECTED DOVER BOOKS
IN ALL FIELDS OF INTEREST

A CATALOGUE OF SELECTED DOVER BOOKS
IN ALL FIELDS OF INTEREST

THE NOTEBOOKS OF LEONARDO DA VINCI, edited by J.P. Richter. Extracts from manuscripts reveal great genius; on painting, sculpture, anatomy, sciences, geography, etc. Both Italian and English. 186 ms. pages reproduced, plus 500 additional drawings, including studies for Last Supper, Sforza monument, etc. 860pp. 7⅞ x 10¾.   USO 22572-0, 22573-9 Pa., Two vol. set $15.90

ART NOUVEAU DESIGNS IN COLOR, Alphonse Mucha, Maurice Verneuil, Georges Auriol. Full-color reproduction of Combinaisons ornamentales (c. 1900) by Art Nouveau masters. Floral, animal, geometric, interlacings, swashes — borders, frames, spots — all incredibly beautiful. 60 plates, hundreds of designs. 9⅜ x 8¹/₁₆ .   22885-1 Pa. $4.00

GRAPHIC WORKS OF ODILON REDON. All great fantastic lithographs, etchings, engravings, drawings, 209 in all. Monsters, Huysmans, still life work, etc. Introduction by Alfred Werner. 209pp. 9⅛ x 12¼.   21996-8 Pa. $6.00

EXOTIC FLORAL PATTERNS IN COLOR, E.-A. Seguy. Incredibly beautiful full-color pochoir work by great French designer of 20's. Complete Bouquets et frondaisons, Suggestions pour étoffes. Richness must be seen to be believed. 40 plates containing 120 patterns. 80pp. 9⅜ x 12¼.   23041-4 Pa. $6.00

SELECTED ETCHINGS OF JAMES A. McN. WHISTLER, James A. McN. Whistler. 149 outstanding etchings by the great American artist, including selections from the Thames set and two Venice sets, the complete French set, and many individual prints. Introduction and explanatory note on each print by Maria Naylor. 157pp. 9⅜ x 12¼.   23194-1 Pa. $5.00

VISUAL ILLUSIONS: THEIR CAUSES, CHARACTERISTICS, AND APPLICATIONS, Matthew Luckiesh. Thorough description, discussion; shape and size, color, motion; natural illusion. Uses in art and industry. 100 illustrations. 252pp.
                                                                        21530-X Pa. $3.00

TEN BOOKS ON ARCHITECTURE, Vitruvius. The most important book ever written on architecture. Early Roman aesthetics, technology, classical orders, site selection, all other aspects. Stands behind everything since. Morgan translation. 331pp.
                                                                        20645-9 Pa. $3.75

THE CODEX NUTTALL. A PICTURE MANUSCRIPT FROM ANCIENT MEXICO, as first edited by Zelia Nuttall. Only inexpensive edition, in full color, of a pre-Columbian Mexican (Mixtec) book. 88 color plates show kings, gods, heroes, temples, sacrifices. New explanatory, historical introduction by Arthur G. Miller. 96pp. 11⅜ x 8½.   23168-2 Pa. $7.50

CREATIVE LITHOGRAPHY AND HOW TO DO IT, Grant Arnold. Lithography as art form: working directly on stone, transfer of drawings, lithotint, mezzotint, color printing; also metal plates. Detailed, thorough. 27 illustrations. 214pp.
21208-4 Pa. $3.50

DESIGN MOTIFS OF ANCIENT MEXICO, Jorge Enciso. Vigorous, powerful ceramic stamp impressions — Maya, Aztec, Toltec, Olmec. Serpents, gods, priests, dancers, etc. 153pp. 6⅛ x 9¼.
20084-1 Pa. $2.50

AMERICAN INDIAN DESIGN AND DECORATION, Leroy Appleton. Full text, plus more than 700 precise drawings of Inca, Maya, Aztec, Pueblo, Plains, NW Coast basketry, sculpture, painting, pottery, sand paintings, metal, etc. 4 plates in color. 279pp. 8⅜ x 11¼.
22704-9 Pa. $5.00

CHINESE LATTICE DESIGNS, Daniel S. Dye. Incredibly beautiful geometric designs: circles, voluted, simple dissections, etc. Inexhaustible source of ideas, motifs. 1239 illustrations. 469pp. 6⅛ x 9¼.
23096-1 Pa. $5.00

JAPANESE DESIGN MOTIFS, Matsuya Co. Mon, or heraldic designs. Over 4000 typical, beautiful designs: birds, animals, flowers, swords, fans, geometric; all beautifully stylized. 213pp. 11⅜ x 8¼.
22874-6 Pa. $5.00

PERSPECTIVE, Jan Vredeman de Vries. 73 perspective plates from 1604 edition; buildings, townscapes, stairways, fantastic scenes. Remarkable for beauty, surrealistic atmosphere; real eye-catchers. Introduction by Adolf Placzek. 74pp. 11⅜ x 8¼.
20186-4 Pa. $3.00

EARLY AMERICAN DESIGN MOTIFS. Suzanne E. Chapman. 497 motifs, designs, from painting on wood, ceramics, appliqué, glassware, samplers, metal work, etc. Florals, landscapes, birds and animals, geometrics, letters, etc. Inexhaustible. Enlarged edition. 138pp. 8⅜ x 11¼.
22985-8 Pa. $3.50
23084-8 Clothbd. $7.95

VICTORIAN STENCILS FOR DESIGN AND DECORATION, edited by E.V. Gillon, Jr. 113 wonderful ornate Victorian pieces from German sources; florals, geometrics; borders, corner pieces; bird motifs, etc. 64pp. 9⅜ x 12¼.
21995-X Pa. $3.00

ART NOUVEAU: AN ANTHOLOGY OF DESIGN AND ILLUSTRATION FROM THE STUDIO, edited by E.V. Gillon, Jr. Graphic arts: book jackets, posters, engravings, illustrations, decorations; Crane, Beardsley, Bradley and many others. Inexhaustible. 92pp. 8⅛ x 11.
22388-4 Pa. $2.50

ORIGINAL ART DECO DESIGNS, William Rowe. First-rate, highly imaginative modern Art Deco frames, borders, compositions, alphabets, florals, insectals, Wurlitzer-types, etc. Much finest modern Art Deco. 80 plates, 8 in color. 8⅜ x 11¼.
22567-4 Pa. $3.50

HANDBOOK OF DESIGNS AND DEVICES, Clarence P. Hornung. Over 1800 basic geometric designs based on circle, triangle, square, scroll, cross, etc. Largest such collection in existence. 261pp.
20125-2 Pa. $2.75

AUSTRIAN COOKING AND BAKING, Gretel Beer. Authentic thick soups, wiener schnitzel, veal goulash, more, plus dumplings, puff pastries, nut cakes, sacher tortes, other great Austrian desserts. 224pp. USO 23220-4 Pa. $2.50

CHEESES OF THE WORLD, U.S.D.A. Dictionary of cheeses containing descriptions of over 400 varieties of cheese from common Cheddar to exotic Surati. Up to two pages are given to important cheeses like Camembert, Cottage, Edam, etc. 151pp. 22831-2 Pa. $1.50

TRITTON'S GUIDE TO BETTER WINE AND BEER MAKING FOR BEGINNERS, S.M. Tritton. All you need to know to make family-sized quantities of over 100 types of grape, fruit, herb, vegetable wines; plus beers, mead, cider, more. 11 illustrations. 157pp. USO 22528-3 Pa. $2.25

DECORATIVE LABELS FOR HOME CANNING, PRESERVING, AND OTHER HOUSEHOLD AND GIFT USES, Theodore Menten. 128 gummed, perforated labels, beautifully printed in 2 colors. 12 versions in traditional, Art Nouveau, Art Deco styles. Adhere to metal, glass, wood, most plastics. 24pp. 8¼ x 11. 23219-0 Pa. $2.00

FIVE ACRES AND INDEPENDENCE, Maurice G. Kains. Great back-to-the-land classic explains basics of self-sufficient farming: economics, plants, crops, animals, orchards, soils, land selection, host of other necessary things. Do not confuse with skimpy faddist literature; Kains was one of America's greatest agriculturalists. 95 illustrations. 397pp. 20974-1 Pa. $3.00

GROWING VEGETABLES IN THE HOME GARDEN, U.S. Dept. of Agriculture. Basic information on site, soil conditions, selection of vegetables, planting, cultivation, gathering. Up-to-date, concise, authoritative. Covers 60 vegetables. 30 illustrations. 123pp. 23167-4 Pa. $1.35

FRUITS FOR THE HOME GARDEN, Dr. U.P. Hedrick. A chapter covering each type of garden fruit, advice on plant care, soils, grafting, pruning, sprays, transplanting, and much more! Very full. 53 illustrations. 175pp. 22944-0 Pa. $2.50

GARDENING ON SANDY SOIL IN NORTH TEMPERATE AREAS, Christine Kelway. Is your soil too light, too sandy? Improve your soil, select plants that survive under such conditions. Both vegetables and flowers. 42 photos. 148pp. USO 23199-2 Pa. $2.50

THE FRAGRANT GARDEN: A BOOK ABOUT SWEET SCENTED FLOWERS AND LEAVES, Louise Beebe Wilder. Fullest, best book on growing plants for their fragrances. Descriptions of hundreds of plants, both well-known and overlooked. 407pp. 23071-6 Pa. $4.00

EASY GARDENING WITH DROUGHT-RESISTANT PLANTS, Arno and Irene Nehrling. Authoritative guide to gardening with plants that require a minimum of water: seashore, desert, and rock gardens; house plants; annuals and perennials; much more. 190 illustrations. 320pp. 23230-1 Pa. $3.50

CATALOGUE OF DOVER BOOKS

COOKIES FROM MANY LANDS, Josephine Perry. Crullers, oatmeal cookies, chaux au chocolate, English tea cakes, mandel kuchen, Sacher torte, Danish puff pastry, Swedish cookies — a mouth-watering collection of 223 recipes. 157pp.
22832-0 Pa. $2.25

ROSE RECIPES, Eleanour S. Rohde. How to make sauces, jellies, tarts, salads, pot-pourris, sweet bags, pomanders, perfumes from garden roses; all exact recipes. Century old favorites. 95pp.
22957-2 Pa. $1.75

"OSCAR" OF THE WALDORF'S COOKBOOK, Oscar Tschirky. Famous American chef reveals 3455 recipes that made Waldorf great; cream of French, German, American cooking, in all categories. Full instructions, easy home use. 1896 edition. 907pp. 6⅝ x 9⅜.
20790-0 Clothbd. $15.00

JAMS AND JELLIES, May Byron. Over 500 old-time recipes for delicious jams, jellies, marmalades, preserves, and many other items. Probably the largest jam and jelly book in print. Originally titled May Byron's Jam Book. 276pp.
USO 23130-5 Pa. $3.50

MUSHROOM RECIPES, André L. Simon. 110 recipes for everyday and special cooking. Champignons à la grecque, sole bonne femme, chicken liver croustades, more; 9 basic sauces, 13 ways of cooking mushrooms. 54pp.
USO 20913-X Pa. $1.25

THE BUCKEYE COOKBOOK, Buckeye Publishing Company. Over 1,000 easy-to-follow, traditional recipes from the American Midwest: bread (100 recipes alone), meat, game, jam, candy, cake, ice cream, and many other categories of cooking. 64 illustrations. From 1883 enlarged edition. 416pp.
23218-2 Pa. $4.00

TWENTY-TWO AUTHENTIC BANQUETS FROM INDIA, Robert H. Christie. Complete, easy-to-do recipes for almost 200 authentic Indian dishes assembled in 22 banquets. Arranged by region. Selected from Banquets of the Nations. 192pp.
23200-X Pa. $2.50

Prices subject to change without notice.
Available at your book dealer or write for free catalogue to Dept. GI, Dover Publications, Inc., 180 Varick St., N.Y., N.Y. 10014. Dover publishes more than 150 books each year on science, elementary and advanced mathematics, biology, music, art, literary history, social sciences and other areas.